COACHING
A TECHNOLOGY FOR CHANGE

A COLLABORATIVE WORK BY PROFESSIONALS
FROM AROUND THE WORLD

FOREWORD BY
JANET HARVEY
Former ICF President

COACHING, A TECHNOLOGY FOR CHANGE

A Collaborative Work by Professionals from Around the World

Copyright 2025 by North Star Success Inc. All Rights Reserved.

For permission requests and bulk orders, please contact support@northstarsuccess.com.

North Star Success Inc. is hereby identified as the owner of this work in accordance with Section 77 of the Copyright, Design and Patents Act 1988.

ISBN: 978-1-0691324-4-4

No part of this publication may be scanned, reproduced, stored in a retrieval system, or transmitted, in any form or by any means, electronic, mechanical, photocopying, recording or otherwise, for public or private use – other than as brief quotations embodied in articles and reviews – without the prior consent of North Star Success Inc. This book is sold subject to the condition that it shall not, by way of trade or otherwise, be lent, resold, hired out or otherwise circulated without North Star Success's prior consent in any form of binding or cover other than that in which it is published.

This is a work of non-fiction. Any resemblance of names, personal characteristics, and details of people, living or dead, is coincidental and unintentional. The authors are responsible for their content and their opinions. AI tools have been used to translate and edit the author-created content. All AI-translated and/or AI-assisted content adheres to all content guidelines.

The reader is solely responsible for their actions and results. If professional or legal advice is required, readers should seek the service of a competent professional. For bulk orders for promotions, fundraising, and educational use, please contact North Star Success Inc. for special discounts. Book excerpts can be created as needed.

Trademark Notice: All brand names and product names used in this book are trademarks, registered trademarks, or trade names of their respective holders. North Star Success Inc. is not associated with any product or vendor mentioned in this book.

Published by North Star Success Inc.

🌐 www.northstarsuccess.com
✉ support@northstarsuccess.com
📞 +1 647 479 0790

Contents

Foreword..7

Introduction..11

Marjan Ashtiani & Mohammadali Shobeiri
Partners in Difference, Allies in Success........................ 21

Farnaz Fakhreddini
The Longing to Be Heard
Active Listening as a Coaching Technology.................. 39

Shahrzad Fakhri
Coaching as a New Approach to Management in
Healthcare Centers 55

Dr. Roya Geravand
Seeking The Truth: A Journey Toward Self-Awareness,
Transformation, and Self-Discovery................................73

Dennis Gharibian
No More Waiting
A Narrative of Change, Self-Awareness, and the Power of Choice
through Coaching...93

Gooya Ghiasi
Whispers of the Soul..109

Azam Iraji
A Woman's Transformation from Teacher to Coach....125

Mohsen Khaki
Coaching as The Unseen Force Behind
High-Performing Leaders..141

Mohammad Mehri
The Third Seat
Where Coaching Takes Flight...163

Dr. Maryam (Elnaz) Rahimzadeh
In Search of the Meaning of Self... 181

Dr. Farinaz Rashedmarandi
Horizons Born of Dreams
Guiding Your Inner Journey...197

Marjan Shams
Seek Within Yourself Whatever You Desire, for It Is You...........215

Nasrin Teimoori
From Teaching to Coaching... 233

Foreword

Our world constantly evolves and presents us with new challenges at every turn. An ability to navigate change with grace and purpose has become a necessity that requires more than skills. As leaders on a path of continuous growth and transformation, we find ourselves at a crossroads, seeking innovative approaches to usher in change effectively and sustainably. Amidst this quest for advancement lies a powerful technology that holds the key to unlocking our full potential and driving meaningful change: coaching, and especially when deployed with a mindset for being generative and authentic.

Imagine for a moment a world where every individual, whether a seasoned executive or a budding entrepreneur, has a trusted companion by their side—someone who empowers them to see beyond the limitations of their current thoughts and beliefs, someone who illuminates the path to their fullest potential. This is the essence of coaching—a transformative journey that transcends mere conversation and delves deep into the realms of self-discovery, growth, and access to internal resources that sustain excellence in every step of continuous change.

Throughout my own personal and professional journey, I have witnessed the profound impact of coaching firsthand. It is not merely a series of sessions or a checklist of tasks; it is a dynamic process that catalyzes growth on a profound internal level. Coaching is the art of asking evocative questions that invite insight versus intellect, of listening intently to uncover hidden truths and what motivates choices, and of inviting individuals toward unique solutions; unique because they come to awareness and then choice, inside-out for each person. Coaching offers a collaborative partnership built on trust, respect, and a shared commitment to relevant growth and the motivation to integrate that growth into a person's worldview, mindset and a chosen, new way of working, leading and living.

One of the most remarkable aspects of coaching is its ability to foster self-awareness—a foundational pillar upon which all personal and professional growth is built. By engaging in deep reflection and introspection facilitated by a skilled coach, individuals gain valuable insights into their beliefs, values, and behaviors. This heightened self-awareness serves as a compass, guiding them towards aligned actions and decisions that propel them towards their goals.

Moreover, coaching serves as a powerful tool for enhancing

communication and interpersonal relationships. Through targeted feedback, active listening, and empathetic questioning, coaches help individuals break down barriers to effective communication and cultivate stronger connections with those around them. Whether navigating conflicts in the boardroom or fostering collaboration within a team, the communication skills honed through coaching are invaluable assets in today's fast-paced and interconnected world that longs deeply for connection and belonging.

Perhaps the greatest gift of coaching lies in its ability to instill a growth mindset—a fundamental belief in one's capacity for continuous learning and development. By challenging limiting beliefs, reframing setbacks as opportunities for discovery and insight, and encouraging experimentation and innovation, coaching nurtures a mindset of adaptability and buoyancy. In a world where change is constant and uncertainty abounds, this mindset serves as a potent antidote to fear and stagnation, empowering individuals to embrace change with courage and optimism.

As the most powerful technology for change, each coaching session reaches beyond a mere conversation, to a sacred space for growth, empowerment and wholeness. Engaging in coaching over time prepares every person to lead self and others as changed individuals, who serve as catalysts for rising to meet change fruitfully, in our organizations and our communities. In the pages that follow, may you discover the transformative

FOREWORD

power of coaching and harness it to drive change in your own life and the lives of those around you. Together, let us embark on this journey of growth, learning, and wholeness, knowing that with coaching as our guide, the possibilities for desirable empowerment and change are limitless.

Janet M. Harvey, CEO inviteCHANGE
ICF Master Certified Coach & Certified Mentor Coach
CSA Accredited Coaching Supervisor

Introduction

Imagine you are sitting with your child, a friend, or an employee, and they say, "I have a problem with procrastination. What should I do?" In this situation, a trainer might introduce the concept of time management. A consultant might offer practical strategies that would help with prioritization. A therapist may investigate underlying causes that may be related to childhood trauma. But if you are a coach, you respond differently: with curiosity, presence, and powerful questions.

You might ask:

- What does procrastination mean to you?
- What's your best guess about what is causing you to procrastinate?
- Can you think of a time when you didn't procrastinate?
- What is different about those times?
- At times when you're inclined to procrastinate, if you consult the best version of yourself, what would you do differently?
- What meaningful value can you activate in yourself that would help you take action when needed?

INTRODUCTION

These questions initiate a deeper process: self-awareness, ownership, and inner transformation. Coaching, in this sense, acts like a technology—a systematic tool designed to bring about change through introspection, clarity, and empowered action.

Coaching as Technology: More Than a Conversation

When we hear "technology," we often think of gadgets and apps. But technology, in its essence, is the application of knowledge for practical purposes. Coaching, then, is a human technology—a structured, evidence-based approach to personal and professional development. It is both art and science, built on frameworks, methodologies, and core competencies designed to facilitate change.

Unlike casual conversations, coaching has structure. It begins with establishing a clear agenda and topic. It continues with deep listening, powerful questioning, exploration of values, and co-creation of actions. It ends with accountability and reflection. And all throughout, there exists a safe and trustful environment. This process is systematic and replicable—just like any well-designed technology.

Why Coaching?

In a world that is constantly changing, individuals and organizations need to adapt, grow, and transform. Coaching provides a reliable, repeatable process to navigate this change. Whether someone is facing burnout, struggling with communication, or seeking clarity on life goals, coaching provides a structured path forward.

Coaching doesn't give prefabricated answers—it helps uncover meaningful customized solutions. In doing so, it respects the client as whole, resourceful, and creative. The coach is not a fixer but a facilitator. And this is what makes coaching profoundly powerful: it honors the autonomy and agency of the individual.

The Anatomy of a Coaching Conversation

What makes coaching different from mentoring or consulting? Consider a business leader struggling with team conflict. A consultant may offer conflict-resolution models. A mentor may share personal experiences. But a coach might ask:

- What outcome do you want from your team?
- What have you tried so far?
- What assumptions are you making about your team members?
- What role are you playing in the conflict?
- What would success look like'?

These questions help the leader reflect, reframe, and reimagine possibilities. Coaching helps to close the gap between current reality and desired outcomes, not by providing answers but by guiding the client to discover their own.

INTRODUCTION

The Evolution of Coaching

While coaching has ancient roots in Socratic dialogue, its modern form has emerged over the last 50 years. In the 1970s, Timothy Gallwey's book, The Inner Game of Tennis, introduced the idea that the "inner game"—the mind's dialogue—was just as important as physical skills. This sparked interest in the psychological aspects of performance.

By the 1990s, coaching had expanded into business and leadership. Influential figures such as Sir John Whitmore and Thomas Leonard formalized coaching into frameworks and professional practices. The International Coaching Federation (ICF) was founded in 1995 to establish global standards, competencies, and ethics.

Today, coaching has spread across industries: from executive coaching to life coaching, health coaching to relationship coaching. Despite its various forms, the core remains the same: a partnership that fosters self-discovery, clarity, and forward momentum.

Coaching's Unique Value Proposition

Coaching is often compared to therapy, mentoring, and consulting. While these professions overlap, each has a unique focus:

- **Therapy** often focuses on healing the past.
- **Mentoring** shares experience and advice.
- **Consulting** provides expert solutions.

- **Coaching** facilitates future-oriented growth and learning.

What sets coaching apart is its emphasis on inquiry over instruction. The coach is not the expert in the client's life—the client is. The coach brings process expertise; the client brings content expertise. This collaborative approach fosters ownership, accountability, and transformation.

Coaching Competencies: The Engine of the Technology

To understand coaching as a technology, consider the core competencies defined by the ICF, which fall into the following broad categories:

- **Co-creating the Relationship:** Establishing trust and intimacy and defining the agenda.
- **Communicating Effectively:** Listening actively and asking powerful questions.
- **Facilitating Learning and Results:** Noticing learning, designing actions, and managing progress.

Each competency is like a gear in a machine. When combined, they produce momentum. A coach who masters these skills creates a reliable, repeatable process for supporting change. This is not random conversation—it is intentional, professional, and evidence-based.

Coaching Outcomes: What the Research Says

The impact of coaching is well-documented. Studies show

that coaching leads to:

- Improved self-confidence (80%)
- Better work performance (70%)
- Enhanced relationships (73%)
- Better communication skills (72%)
- Increased wellness and reduced stress

Organizations report return on investment (ROI) from coaching as high as 500–700%. But beyond statistics, the real impact of coaching is qualitative: clients feel more seen, heard, and empowered. They gain new perspectives. They take bold action. [1]

The Ethics and Professionalism of Coaching

Because coaching is currently an unregulated field, standards matter. That's why accreditation through bodies like ICF or European Mentoring and Coaching Council (EMCC) is critical. Certified coaches commit to continuous learning, supervision, and adherence to ethical guidelines.

Just as you wouldn't trust an unlicensed doctor, professional coaching demands proper training. This includes:

- Mastering competencies
- Practicing with real clients
- Receiving mentor coaching

---

1. International Coaching Federation. (2023). 2023 ICF global coaching study: Executive summary. https://coachingfederation.org/resource/global-coaching-study-executive-summary-2023/

- Passing credentialing exams

This structure ensures that coaching remains not just a conversation—but a credible, impactful intervention.

Who Needs Coaching?

The better question is: who doesn't? Coaching is for:

- Leaders seeking greater impact
- Teams striving for collaboration
- Individuals pursuing life goals
- Parents navigating change
- Entrepreneurs managing uncertainty

Anyone facing transition, complexity, or a desire for growth can benefit from coaching. It's not about fixing what's broken. It's about optimizing what's possible.

The Future of Coaching

As the world becomes more complex and interconnected, coaching is more relevant than ever. It is being integrated into:

- Organizational development
- Health care and mental wellness
- Education and youth empowerment
- Technology and AI platforms

Coaching is becoming a leadership style, a communication skill, and a way of being. It's not just for coaches—it's for anyone who wants to lead with empathy, ask better questions, and create space for growth.

Becoming a Coach: The Journey Begins

If you feel called to become a coach, start with proper training. Choose a program accredited by the ICF or another reputable body. Look for a curriculum that includes:

- Deep instruction on core competencies
- Emphasis on the ICF code of ethics
- Live practicums
- Mentor coaching
- Feedback and assessment
- A community of peers

But becoming a coach is more than checking boxes. It's a personal journey. It requires:

- Deep self-reflection
- Courage to hold space
- Commitment to ethics
- A learner's mindset

Great coaches are not born—they are developed. And the journey itself is transformational.

Conclusion: Coaching as a Technology for the Human Spirit

We live in an age of disruption, but also of possibility. In this context, coaching is not a luxury—it's a necessity. It equips individuals and organizations to navigate change, build resilience, and thrive.

Coaching is a technology for transformation. Not one made of wires and circuits—but of presence and purpose, curiosity and courage. It is a bridge from where we are to where we want to be.

And it all begins with a question: **How do you want to show up in challenging situations?**

Dr. Shahab Anari
ICF Master Coach (MCC),
Founder of North Star Coach Training Program

Partners in Difference, Allies in Success

Marjan Ashtiani
Mohammadali Shobeiri

Partners in Difference, Allies in Success

Marjan Ashtiani
Financial Markets Analyst, Professional Trader, Trading Psychology Coach, and Founder of LunariaFX

Mohammadali Shobeiri
Strategist, Professional Coach, and Organizational Growth Architect in the Petrochemical Industry

> We are two rivers, born of two mountains, seeking to become the sea.
> Our dream will be realized the moment we become 'Us.'
> You are filled with dreams of taking flight, while I think of the homeland.
> You are ready for the journey; I long to share our story.
> At times, in the rapids of doubt, we were cast far apart,
> But once more, a light shone deep within our souls.
> Not alike in appearance, but kindred in spirit,
> Like a melody and a voice, or like the moonlight and the air.

For centuries, humanity has relied on an unwritten law for survival: eat or be eaten. However, in human relationships—especially in the twenty-first century—this logic is not only ineffective but destructive. Today, the fundamental question is not about which of us gets to remain, but rather how we can stay together and grow despite our differences. For me, the question has always been: Why do some couples, amidst profound differences, not only endure but flourish together? I found the answer years later in our own story—the story of Marjan and me. Our story isn't just about a relationship; it is a testament to the truth that a bond can be formed in the heart of conflict—a bond that grows not on the foundation of similarity but on acceptance, dialogue, and collaboration. We walked two different paths: Marjan was in love with the dynamic ecosystem of global startups, while I was rooted in the industries of Iran. She envisioned new futures in distant lands; I was invested in building tomorrow on the familiar soil of my homeland. Yet, amid all these differences, something held us together: a shared belief in individual progress within a mature relationship.

What we built was not a relationship where one had to be sacrificed for the other to shine. We chose to find a path to shine together. We write this chapter to show that personal growth and professional success do not have to come at the expense of a loving relationship—on one condition: that we learn not to fight our differences, but to build strength from them. For this purpose, just like what we do in coaching, we learned to ask each other powerful questions, hold space for difficult truths, and define our values. We discovered that the most effective 'technology for change' wasn't in our industries, but in the quality of our dialogue. The audience for this chapter includes anyone who has ever felt torn by the timeless dilemma of success versus love. Those who believe that to advance, they must sacrifice their relationship, or conversely, that to preserve their relationship, they must give up on their dreams. We assert: No! It is possible to have both if we learn how to communicate, understand each other's paths, and know when to be patient and when to walk alongside each other, even if our paths diverge.

Like many, we often found ourselves at crossroads where one path seemed to lead to "Me" and the other to "Us." Each time, we sought to forge a third path: one that preserved the "Us" without erasing the "Me." This narrative is for those who believe in dialogue, who are eager to collaborate in building rather than sacrificing, and who seek to create a true balance between intimacy and independence. Through difficult decisions, career crises, and nights filled with doubt, Marjan and I learned that no relationship grows on its own; it must be nurtured every day. We must remain honest in crisis, supportive in success, and expansive in difference. We didn't intend to be the narrators of *my* story or *Marjan's* story. Instead, we chose to view ourselves from both perspectives, like the omniscient narrator of a novel. A third-person narrative! As if we were sitting impartially on the sidelines, recounting the story—just that, free of judgment.

Between Two Dreams, in the Heart of a Choice

On a spring morning, the house was filled with a silence brimming with unspoken energy. Not the absence of words, but the calm before a storm. Marjan paced the living room, a cup of coffee still untouched in her hand, her mind a whirlwind of unspoken thoughts and a nameless feeling. On the other side of the room, Mohammadali turned over his phone, casting a brief but heavy glance at the news that could change his entire future: an offer to manage one of the country's largest petrochemical companies. A few hours earlier, Marjan had received an email: a formal invitation from another European country to join the founding team of an innovative startup. The dream she had nurtured for years was now on the verge of becoming a reality. But the expected joy never came. Instead, doubt, a form of nameless anxiety, and a vague sadness took hold. They were both on the cusp of achieving their greatest professional dreams, yet their aspirations were not aligned.

A storm raged in Marjan's heart that she couldn't articulate. She had prepared for this moment for years, but now that it had arrived, why didn't she feel liberated? Her gaze kept drifting to Mohammadali. If she left, what would happen to "Us"? If she stayed, what would happen to her? Mohammadali was not at peace either. Outwardly calm and composed, he was a dormant volcano inside. The career position he had always dreamed of was now before him as a formal offer. But what about Marjan? If she left, if the distance between them grew, would their love survive? Should one of them step back so the other could shine? Or was there a way to stay together without one becoming a sacrifice? The nights grew longer, and their silences heavier. Words remained stuck in their throats, and only their eyes spoke. Marjan took refuge in her ever-present journal. For years, that notebook had been a sanctuary for words too heavy to share with others. Now, she wrote of fear, longing, and the homesickness she felt even before leaving. Mohammadali chose aimless night drives, with soft music and a sky without stars. For him, these moments were a quiet prelude to life's great decisions.

Finally, the decision was made. Marjan left. Mohammadali stayed. Not with heartbreak or anger, but with a deep acceptance: sometimes, love means letting go with faith. Sometimes, it means giving permission to fly, even if you remain on the ground. But the distance was not easy. For Marjan, the feeling of being away was not just geographical; it was psychological and emotional as well. Work challenges, cultural differences, competition, financial pressure, and loneliness surrounded her. Mohammadali, too, amidst massive industrial projects, felt as though he had left a part of himself behind. He kept the true depth of his loneliness to himself, sharing it with neither his colleagues nor his own thoughts. He found solace only on quiet nights, with a cold cup of tea and a blank page before him.

Yet, they had made a pact: a commitment to transparency and unmasked dialogue. Gradually, habits formed: regular calls, heartfelt emails, and notes exchanged between them. They learned that although their bodies were far apart, their hearts could remain in sync—if they both desired it, if honesty was their common language.

Despite the hardships, they moved forward until they reached a new crossroads. Marjan's startup had hit a dead end; the capital was gone, and her energy depleted. Mohammadali no longer felt passion for his industrial projects, and his professional smiles could no longer hide the fatigue in his eyes. They seemed to be standing strong, but inside, something had crumbled. For weeks, a heavy silence flowed between them—not anger or resentment, but a profound quiet that demanded only presence. Occasionally, one would ask, "Was it worth it?" and the other wouldn't answer, as there was no simple response. Marjan returned to her journal, where her words now reflected exhaustion—of misplaced expectations that left her feeling emptier instead of successful. Yet, among these bitter sentences, seeds of hope began to sprout: a new perspective on herself, her capabilities, and the meaning she could bring to others, even on a small scale.

This time, there was no major crisis; no email invitation or exciting offer. Only a quiet night, with soft rain tapping against the window and the scent of wet earth filling the air. In the silence, Mohammadali softly said, "Marjan... I can't see myself on this path anymore. Everything feels colorless. Maybe it's time to build a new world. Together, not apart."

Marjan paused. Her calm gaze met Mohammadali's. It was familiar, but something had changed—like a reflection of herself after all this time. She said quietly, "Me too... I don't want to build alone anymore. I don't want to return to the big ideas of the past. I want to start with you, even if nothing is certain. From zero, but together. I want to build something small, not for winning, just for meaning. Even in a storm, even in hell, a paradise can be built!"

In that moment, everything changed. Not suddenly, but like flipping a switch; a small spark, full of hope. They no longer had to prove anything to anyone—not to family, society, or even themselves. For the first time, their decision was rooted in a shared sense of peace, not in grand ambition or external dreams.

Tired of being apart and wanting to be with her, Mohammadali quietly submitted his resignation. His heart was no longer in petrochemicals, charts, and budgets. He had received a new offer to teach and mentor in personal development. Something inside him whispered, "Maybe it's time to use your past as a tool for the future." His gaze, the same one Marjan had fallen in love with years ago, was full of affection, tears, and determination.

A Joint Flight

They decided to immigrate together this time. Mohammadali gave up his hard-fought position in the petrochemical industry, and Marjan closed her solo startup chapter. A few months later, they arrived in a new country. The language was unfamiliar, the streets strange, and even the sky's color was different. For the first time, they faced the unknown together, and their shared strangeness became their greatest asset. The beginning was tough; they faced nights without money, days of uncertainty, and creeping doubts. Sometimes, they wondered if they had made a mistake. Yet, during those dark nights, the foundations of their joint company were laid. Their idea was simple: to combine their strengths in an educational and consulting firm, merging Mohammadali's industrial experience with Marjan's communication and cultural skills. This time, their dream was to make a meaningful impact in people's lives.

They sat together at night, drafting business plans, crossing things out, and starting over. Sometimes they felt frustrated; at other times, disheartened. But neither let go—not when the investor didn't come, not when their collaborators quit, and not even when weeks passed without a positive response. Then the day came when the contract for their first project was signed. There was no celebration—just a smile exchanged between Marjan and Mohammadali.

Marjan said, "I feel like we're truly building together. Not out of fear or need, but choice." Mohammadali smiled, embracing the moment. They understood that success isn't just about numbers; sometimes, it finds meaning in creating a small but sincere world.

Life became simpler—perhaps with fewer resources, but with more peace. At night, they sat together, needing few words—sometimes just silence, a few lines from a book, or a thank-you email from a client. These small things carried profound meaning. On this path, they learned that success, though different from their old dreams, became more real because it was rooted in their togetherness. Through all the differences, challenges, and failures, what remained was a love redefined every day.

The Dance Between Hope and Despair: A Victory Anthem in Silence

Life is never a straight line; it is more like a melody that oscillates between silence and excitement, doubt and faith. Marjan and Mohammadali's joint company reflected that melody. Sometimes it soared, sometimes it dipped, but it always had a living voice: the sound of "being together." In the beginning, projects were few. Marjan held small courses for immigrant youth and women—open discussion sessions and workshops on identity and empowerment. She didn't have a large team or significant capital, but each time she drew a smile of satisfaction from a weary woman or inspired a young girl with renewed courage, she felt she was on the right path. Perhaps the distance had taught them that to grow, they could stay together and build together.

In a small room, Mohammadali held career coaching sessions for immigrants, confused youth, and exhausted employees who had hit a dead end. Progress was slow but meaningful. The classes were small, yet the looks that followed him at the end of each session conveyed a sense of affirmation and respect. He, too, learned that meaning isn't necessarily found in national projects; sometimes, it is encapsulated in changing the course of a single human life. Marjan would occasionally meet a woman who could barely speak, but after a few sessions, she would begin to develop her own ideas. Mohammadali would sometimes receive an email weeks after consulting with a hopeless man: "Thank you for reminding me that I can start again."

Success was now defined by smiles. It was made up of simple words like "hope," "courage," and "I finally started." There were no more grand halls or glossy logos, but a deep satisfaction had settled in their hearts—something they had been seeking for years. Marjan still kept her journal, but now she wrote about the feeling of being useful—not the anxiety of separation or the tears of loneliness, but short stories of women who had transformed. Mohammadali no longer took nighttime drives to escape his thoughts; now, his nights provided a space to contemplate the future—a future that had taken shape, not perfect or flawless, but real.

One evening after work, Marjan thought, "We were supposed to start from zero. What a warm and fruitful 'zero' it was!" Mohammadali was thinking the same thing: they hadn't started from zero; they had started from *themselves*.

In this chapter of their lives, they learned that hope and despair are like two sides of the same coin, and only someone who knows how to harmonize with another—not compete—can build hope from the ashes of despair. Their relationship was no longer a battleground for two dreams but a dance floor for two people—in balance, in silence, in a harmony they had fought for years. They had learned that when love is real, it neither consumes nor diminishes you. Love, when it is a companion, fosters growth, gives meaning to your identity, and adds soul to your work. This new path wasn't a story of success; it was a story of building.

Their goal was to create something shared, human, and real in a world that constantly pulls people apart. Marjan and Mohammadali had rediscovered that love, commitment, and dreams can walk hand in hand, without one being sacrificed for the other, forging a clear path even amidst uncertainty.

The Coaching Principles We Lived By

Looking back today, we realize our life's journey has been full of ups and downs. It would have been easier for one of us to prioritize ourselves and chase our own dreams. But we wanted that dream alongside the person we love and the person who loves us. Just like a family dinner! Whether the food is lavish or simple, being together makes everything more enjoyable. Neither of us accepted the role of victim. We did not set aside our own dreams to build the other's; instead, we built a new, purposeful, and valuable dream together.

Our journey was powered not by abstract theories but by the powerful principles of coaching. A commitment to unmasked safe dialogue and shared visioning allowed us to co-create our future, while a resilient mindset gave us the strength to reframe failure. This empowered us to reject binary choices and forge a 'third path'—an integrative solution built on our deepest values.

Partners in Difference, Allies in Success

About the Authors

Marjan Ashtiani is a financial markets analyst, professional trader, trading psychology coach, and the founder of **LunariaFX**. She is a multifaceted and influential figure in the trading world, having pioneered a new approach to trading education and coaching by blending analytical perspectives, psychological approaches, and real-world market experience. Her expertise in the Forex market and the Iranian stock exchange, along with the development of two unique methods, **T3** and **RSI3**, has established an independent and practical educational platform. Over the past year, this platform has been redesigned and its content upgraded, making it one of the primary resources for professional training in the field.

Before entering the financial world, Marjan studied Civil Engineering and worked for many years on large-scale civil projects, particularly in project control, design, and execution. She now leverages her extensive skills in network-based programming to provide a more precise perspective on analytical and systemic trading structures.

Recently, her areas of activity have expanded to include services such as trading coaching, business model design, and the preparation of technical-economic studies for projects. Her latest international endeavor is the establishment of her company's second branch in the UAE—a strategic move to enhance her personal brand and professional activities at a regional level.

Marjan is not just a market professional; she is a multidimensional individual who, while advancing in her professional fields, has also dedicated herself to studying child development with a cognitive and humanistic approach, demonstrating exceptional brilliance and commitment in her role as a mother.

In the media and on social networks, she presents an approachable and sincere persona.

Inspirational, her goal is to support those who wish to think more consciously, act more independently, and build their financial and personal paths with self-confidence.

Partners in Difference, Allies in Success

About the Authors

Mohammadali Shobeiri is a strategist, professional coach, and organizational growth architect in the petrochemical industry. He is a prominent and influential figure in the fields of strategic management and business development in Iran. With a background in civil engineering, Mohammadali furthered his professional credentials by completing a Master of Business Administration (MBA) and a Doctorate of Business Administration (DBA). He continued his academic path by earning a PhD in Management from Université Clermont Auvergne in France, combining his field experience with analytical knowledge to become a trusted authority in strategic leadership.

He has served as a Strategic Manager at one of the country's largest petrochemical companies, where he has played a key role in the development and implementation of several petrochemical plants. His expertise in drafting economic feasibility studies and designing business models for large corporations has earned him recognition as the nation's top strategy manager in national assessments for several consecutive years.

In addition to his organizational activities, Mohammadali is a professional coach certified by the International Coaching Federation (ICF). He focuses on personal growth, leadership development, and strategic decision-making, guiding managers and entrepreneurs on their paths to progress. His approach to strategic coaching is deeply informed by his personal journey of navigating complex career transitions and building a life centered on shared values.

Contact the Authors:

Marjan:
- +971522340076
- +971522340076
- lunariafx (https://t.mc/lunariafx)
- marjan.t.ashtiani@gmail.com and lunariafx@gmail.com

Mohammadali:
- +971582340076
- +971582340076
- Mohammadali.coach@gmail.com

Company:

📷 mascoadvisory
✉ mascoadvisory@gmail.com
🌐 www.mascoadvisory.com

The Longing to Be Heard
Active Listening as a Coaching Technology

Farnaz Fakhreddini

The Longing to Be Heard
Active Listening as a Coaching Technology

Farnaz Fakhreddini
Instructor and Coach for Self-Discovery and Effective Communication

As he introduced himself, his round, dark eyes darted around the room, stealing glances at me while avoiding direct eye contact. I asked, "Are you feeling uncomfortable? Would you prefer me to turn off the video and continue our conversation over the phone?"

Swiftly and with resolute confidence, he replied, "No!" Then, after a brief pause, he admitted, "This is the first time I've had a video conversation with a lady."

These were the opening words of my first session with Aman, a thirteen-year-old boy from Bushehr, south of Iran. He was my first adolescent client, and I must confess, I was just so eager for this session. Having no prior experience with teenage clients, I was keen to understand his motivation for seeking coaching.

In an introductory coaching session, the discussion typically revolves around the structure, methodology, general framework, and regulations of the sessions. Once we reach a mutual agreement, the subsequent meetings are scheduled. As I carefully tried to explain these aspects in a comprehensible and straightforward manner, he suddenly interrupted me upon hearing the word "listening" and asked, "Does this mean I will have to speak, and you will listen?" His question made me ponder. What did he truly mean? Our initial session evolved into an intriguing exchange that sparked questions for both of us. Later, I learned from his own words that he had been just as eager for this session as I was. I sincerely hoped he would agree to continue so our sessions could formally begin. After my explanations, he simply said, "I accept. Let's begin."

I smiled and responded, "Aman, we need to coordinate the date and time for our first session. You have schoolwork to attend to, and I have other sessions and commitments. Please let me know your availability so we can establish a fixed schedule for twelve sessions."

Upon hearing the number twelve, he inquired, "Does this mean I will have twelve sessions with you? I will talk, and you will listen to me?"

After finalizing the details, our first session commenced. As the video call connected, I briefly thought someone else had joined the meeting. But soon, I realized it was Aman himself. He sat in a neatly arranged, pleasant environment, dressed smartly, and, as he later mentioned, had even visited the barber to prepare himself for the occasion.

Seeing him, I felt a deep sense of joy. I said, "Aman, I am listening."

He responded, "What? Are you listening? No one has ever said that to me before."

He then began his story: "You see, no one, from my parents to my siblings, even my teachers and acquaintances, listens to me. They hear my voice, but nothing more. My voice is acknowledged only when I answer a question in class, play with my friends, or do household chores. I have so much to say, and I long for someone who will truly listen to me."

The Importance of Listening

In our subsequent sessions, Aman spoke with an enthusiasm that seemed to fill the space around him. It was then that I fully grasped the significance of his initial question: "Does this mean I will have to speak, and you will listen?"

By breaking the silence of his inner world, this endearing thirteen-year-old boy began to reveal the challenges he had endured, the thoughts he had never shared, and the burdens he had carried alone. Time and again, he would ask, "Can I keep speaking?" Each time I nodded, his dark eyes would light up, and he would pour his heart into every word. His gratitude for being truly heard was evident in his expressions, the sparkle in his eyes, and the joy resonating in his voice. During one session, when he hesitated and asked if he had been talking too much, I gently inquired, "Why do you ask that?"

He cast a tentative glance at me, and with a lowered gaze and somber tone, he replied, "Because no one has ever listened to me before."

I asked, "Why didn't they?"

"I don't know," he replied. "Maybe they were tired, busy, bored, or angry. All I know is that they just didn't listen."

As our eleventh session drew to a close, having addressed the challenges he had brought forth, I asked him for feedback—what his takeaway from these sessions had been, what added value they had provided for him, and what he intended to learn from them.

We had scheduled our meeting for Sunday at 5 p.m. Aman confessed that, from 3 p.m. onward, he had not taken his eyes off the clock or his phone, feeling as though every minute dragged on like an hour.

I asked, "Why?"

He pulled out a small notebook and said, "Because of this!"

I had posed three questions, expecting no more than a few lines in response. To my surprise, he handed me an entire notebook brimming with thoughtful reflections. His dedication and meticulousness warmed my heart. Clearly, Aman had taken the time to ponder deeply and articulate his thoughts with care.

Impressed, I asked, "Aman, what inspired you to write so much?"

He replied, "For a long time, I never spoke about myself- my problems, desires, dreams, and wishes. Not because I didn't want to, but because I had no one I could truly trust. Even when I tried, they wouldn't listen. Perhaps they heard my voice, but their attention was always somewhere else. They would be distracted, doing other things, merely pretending to listen. Or worse, they'd cut me off before I finished speaking to offer advice or blame—something I absolutely detest. I grew weary of hearing phrases like 'Do this,' 'Don't say that,' 'It's for your own good,' and 'This is better for your future.' All these endless rules and restrictions made me regret ever speaking at all. So, I remained silent until I found someone who would genuinely listen without judgment."

I then asked, "Alright, Aman, what happened to your answers to my questions?"

He asked, "Should I read them aloud? Do you have the patience to listen?" and with a playful smile, he added, "Oh, I know! You will listen to me patiently. Just as you have throughout the past eleven sessions."

And so, he began reading from his notebook, opening with these heartfelt words: "Thank you for listening to me."

His words touched me deeply, making me ponder: why should anyone be denied the freedom to express themselves? Why do we so often fail to truly listen? I have met only one Aman, but there are countless others like him—perhaps even ourselves.

Aman's closing words held profound meaning for me, making our final session a moment etched into memory: "When someone listens to you, you no longer feel alone. That was the greatest gift you gave me."

Active Listening: The Key to Effective Communication

Active listening transcends the mere act of hearing words; it demands full attention, understanding, and a genuine interest in the speaker's thoughts. It is the bedrock of meaningful communication. When we listen with intent, we impart a powerful message—a sense of value and recognition: "I see you. You matter to me."

Dale Carnegie, in his celebrated book *How to Win Friends and Influence People,* captures this truth beautifully: "Listening to others is a form of respect."[1]

This led me to ponder my own preferences: How do I wish to be heard? Would I seek approval? Would I welcome interruptions filled with unsolicited advice or judgments? Or would I long for something greater—an unspoken promise to truly listen?

More often than not, my deepest yearning is to be truly heard, not merely my words, but the emotions interwoven with them, the unspoken thoughts that reside in the corners of my mind and weigh silently upon my heart.

I ideally prefer the person sitting across from me to be fully attentive and focused on my words, setting aside distractions such as mobile phones, and listening to me without judgment or preconceived notions. To ensure a clear understanding of

---

1. Carnegie, D. (1936). *How to win friends and influence people.* Simon & Schuster.

my intent, they should ask clarifying questions to prevent any misunderstandings. They could then repeat or summarize my words to demonstrate their attentiveness while showing interest in my thoughts through body language, such as maintaining eye contact, nodding, or using other gestures. With patience and composure, they should allow me to speak freely and express my emotions, fostering a sense of trust and understanding.

When I put myself in the client's shoes and reflected on how I would prefer to be listened to, I realized that listening not only helps me understand others better but also enables them to gain a deeper understanding of themselves.

Active listening provides clarity regarding problems and challenges, allowing us to devise more effective solutions. It fosters the acquisition of new knowledge and broadens our perspectives. By actively listening, we can avoid misunderstandings that might lead to conflicts and disputes. When I listen attentively to my interlocutor, I help boost their self-confidence, reduce their stress and anxiety, and potentially empower them to discover new solutions, generate creative ideas, or simply achieve a positive state of mind.

Let us remember that active listening is a skill that develops and improves with practice. Through consistent effort, we can become more active and effective listeners.

Do You Listen to Your Inner Voice?

This question is essential, as its answer unlocks the path to deeper self-understanding. Each of us has an inner voice—a part of our being that we often neglect. This voice reflects our emotions, desires, needs, and inner calling. But how often do we truly pay attention to it?

Our inner voice is a fundamental aspect of who we are. Yet how much attention do we truly give to it? We must recognize that it can sometimes operate automatically, adopting a critical or negative tone, while at other times, it serves as a positive and supportive presence. There are moments when it may seem to fade away entirely. At its best, this voice can be kind and wise; at its worst, it can be our harshest critic, condemning our every action.

For instance, under stress, we often allow our minds to wander and focus on external events instead of our inner world. This shift can lead to rigidity and negativity in our thoughts, causing us to react impulsively rather than think critically.

For centuries, philosophers have sought to understand and define the inner voice. However, it was not until 1993 that this concept was formally examined from a psychological perspective, thanks to a study conducted by Hubert Hermans and Harry Kempen at Radboud University Nijmegen in the Netherlands.[1] Their research revealed that the inner voice can be harnessed for reasoning and contemplating the realities around us. Essentially, it represents a form of introspection that helps us understand and connect with our surroundings.

---

1. Hermans, H. J. M., & Kempen, H. J. G. (1993). The dialogical self: Meaning as movement. *The American Journal of Psychology,* 107(4).

Building on this foundation, in the late 1990s, scientists began to explore the inner voice more deeply as a psychological phenomenon. To date, they have gathered compelling evidence suggesting that this mental process serves valuable psychological purposes, such as planning, problem-solving, reflection, and self-awareness.

Essential Tools for Hearing the Inner Voice

Meditation facilitates an inward journey, allowing us to truly listen to our inner voice. Both meditation and mindfulness are powerful tools that help us recognize and connect with this voice. By creating a space of silence and tranquility, meditation frees the mind from the noise of daily thoughts, enabling us to perceive the subtle and often overlooked voice within. When the mind is calm, intrusive thoughts diminish, allowing us to focus more clearly on our emotions and intuition.

Meditation and mindfulness heighten our awareness of thoughts, emotions, and physical sensations. This increased awareness helps us identify and understand our thought patterns and emotional responses. Through consistent practice, we can learn to distinguish between our authentic inner voice and those influenced by fear, anxiety, or negativity. Stress and anxiety can muffle the inner voice, preventing us from hearing it. By alleviating these tensions, meditation calms the mind and creates the necessary space to connect with one's inner voice. Additionally, meditation enhances our focus, enabling us to pay attention to our inner voice while avoiding distractions.

Types of Meditation for Hearing the Inner Voice

- **Mindfulness Meditation:** This practice allows us to observe our thoughts and emotions without judgment.
- **Mantra Meditation:** Repeating a specific word or phrase can calm the mind and focus our attention on the inner voice.
- **Visualization Meditation:** Imagining peaceful scenes or settings helps establish a connection with the subconscious, allowing us to hear our inner voice.

Through consistent meditation and mindfulness practices, we can deepen our connection with ourselves and embrace the wise guidance of our inner voice.

The Inner Voice: A Hidden Treasure

Listening to the inner voice is a personal journey. Writing about our feelings and thoughts enhances our understanding of them, while immersing ourselves in nature fosters calmness and improves our ability to hear our inner voice. Each individual has a unique way of connecting with their inner self. The key is to take the first step and trust this voice within. By listening to our inner voice, we gain greater self-awareness and a deeper understanding of our strengths and weaknesses. When we follow this inner call, we make better choices in life's critical decisions.

It is essential to listen to and nurture the inner voice. In truth, it is the best companion we can have on the journey of life, as it enables us to be more attuned to our surroundings and emotions.

To truly hear ourselves—and others—is not just an act of connection, but a quiet revolution that begins with presence, patience, and the courage to listen deeply.

The Longing to Be Heard
Active Listening as a Coaching Technology

About the Author

Farnaz Fakhreddini, a life coach and instructor, has embarked on a journey full of ups and downs in the path of self-awareness and personal growth. She had a passion for learning and teaching since childhood. After graduating in chemistry, she spent years working in the field of laboratory equipment and education, but fate called her to a different path. Life changes introduced Farnaz to the world of self-awareness and consciousness. She spent six years studying, teaching, and experiencing self-awareness and consciousness. Then she started to hold courses on Enneagram personality recognition and self-awareness with a focus on the analysis of reciprocal behavior.

She then became familiar with coaching, and this opportunity opened a new door to her world of personal growth and development. Farnaz, utilizing her knowledge and experience, helps her clients discover their life values, improve their relationships, and achieve their goals. She accompanies individuals toward self-awareness and personal growth by holding in-person and online coaching sessions. Currently, as a growth and flourishing specialist, Farnaz is designing and teaching various personal development skills courses.

Her motto is: "Find yourself, build your life, and change your world." Farnaz's interest in yoga and meditation shows that she pays attention to different dimensions of human existence. By combining her knowledge and experience in various fields, she helps people live conscious, purposeful, and satisfying lives.

Ways to contact the author:

 farnaz.fakhreddini
 +98-9123220130
 +44-7950720957
 Farnaz Fakhreddini
 www.Can-DoCoaching.com
 fakhreddinifarnaz@gmail.com

Coaching as a New Approach to Management in Healthcare Centers

Shahrzad Fakhri

Coaching as a New Approach to Management in Healthcare Centers

Shahrzad Fakhri

The First Organizational Coach for Medical Laboratories

Throughout our professional journeys, we encounter moments that challenge us not just in our careers but internally as well. These are times when we question whether we are aligned with our beliefs or merely conforming to organizational duties.

Have you ever felt overwhelmed by heavy responsibilities without receiving adequate support from your organization? In such situations, communicating with others, maintaining team morale, and staying on course become complex challenges.

What do you do when your goals do not align with the organization's direction? To what extent do you believe in a shared vision?

Does your organization provide the necessary space to express your ideas, criticisms, and pursue personal growth, or must you remain silent to survive?

In this chapter, you will explore a story set in the world of healthcare, where sensitivity, commitment, and responsibility are of utmost importance. What do you think distinguishes working in healthcare from other industries?

If you can answer all these questions clearly, congratulations! However, if you hesitate to respond to even one, it may be time to consider the role of coaching in organizational leadership, especially in healthcare.

The Birth of a Quest: A Personal Experience in Healthcare Centers

I started working in pathobiology laboratories in 1997. Throughout the years, as I worked in different medical centers, I was consistently recognized as a dedicated, responsible, and impactful professional. Along the way, I encountered many challenges, conflicts, and inefficiencies—experiences that helped me uncover the root causes behind the setbacks and lack of sustainable growth in small and mid-sized healthcare centers.

My professional career began in a mid-sized laboratory. Driven by high motivation and grand ambitions, I decided to further my education. While continuing my studies, I worked as a supervisor in various departments, and my capabilities and performance quickly led to more and more responsibilities. However, to my surprise, this increase was not accompanied by fair financial growth. A sense of injustice and exploitation began to form within me: Why should I work harder and have more responsibilities than others, but not receive more in return?

The Bitterness of Hollow Promises

In one of the laboratories, the management, aiming to expand the center, launch new departments, and turn it into an infertility center, invited me to collaborate more seriously and promised an improved job position and higher income—a proposal that aligned with my enthusiasm for growth. I decided to leave my job at the hospital. I submitted my resignation to the hospital laboratory manager, but it was met with strong opposition. I was promised better conditions, but when I insisted on my decision, they reluctantly accepted my resignation. I left my job and embarked on a new path.

Just one month after starting my new job at the laboratory, everything went contrary to expectations. The promised salary was not paid, and when I inquired about it, this was the response: "The value of your work is much higher than these amounts, but we are currently unable to pay!"

A deep sense of insecurity developed within me. I had lost my previous job, my former boss was upset with me, and I didn't know what to do with my passion for growth and progress.

The Weight of Unseen Burdens

At the beginning of my career, I grappled with mental obstacles, including the fear of unemployment and anxiety about the future. Although I didn't know where to go, my eagerness to grow surpassed my fear. Despite my criticisms of management, I poured my heart into my work. Patients were satisfied, test results were accurate and timely, and my performance was really good. However, at the end of each year, a sense of insecurity would overwhelm me. In annual evaluations, I only saw the laboratory's progress, not my own. I felt that my love for service and passion for growth were being utilized without bringing me inner satisfaction.

Every year, I considered leaving my job, but promises and reassurances consistently kept me from making that change.

As the laboratory was growing, so was the workload. I was in charge of all the various responsibilities—from ordering kits and equipment to managing inventory, handling repairs, controlling inbound and outbound flow, providing customer service, facilitating internal communications, and managing crises. Despite this significant volume of responsibility, I not only lacked job satisfaction but also felt emotionally exhausted.

Team or Group? I Felt the Difference

Years later, I realized the profound difference between a "team" and a "group." We were merely a group gathered to achieve an economic goal, not a team striving for a higher, shared objective. Management seemed more focused on the dream of development than genuinely working toward it. My sense of insecurity multiplied as I no longer shared a common goal with my colleagues. While income was essential to me, it was not my ultimate goal. I felt that my objectives were misaligned with those of management. I endured difficult days, caught in ambiguity and unsure which decisions were correct. Reflecting on that period today, I wonder why I waited so long for management to address my needs.

The plans only existed on paper, and the meetings were filled with the same repetitive promises. This was distressing for me, as I had a strong inner motivation to learn and acquire knowledge. When I requested permission to attend training courses and share my learnings with colleagues afterward, I faced opposition. My question was: "Shouldn't an organization that wants to grow welcome the growth and learning of its staff?"

Decision to Change

Amidst feelings of exploitation, I decided to continue my education. On Thursdays and Fridays, my mind was filled with concerns, insecurity, ambiguity, and unanswered questions as I attended classes to prepare for Master's degree entrance exam while also addressing employee dissatisfaction with wages. It was difficult to hide my own pain while urging my colleagues to remain calm and adaptable. Those around me mistakenly assumed I was one of the shareholders of the center, when in reality, I was merely a hardworking individual with aspirations to build. These pressures sometimes caused me to behave harshly toward my subordinates.

Rather than questioning my reactions or exploring their underlying causes, the manager chose to criticize my behavior toward employees. Moreover, managers made arbitrary decisions regarding certain requirements, leading to serious disagreements. I often heard the response, "You are too strict!" However, I had a different perspective; I believed that the healthcare field, like driving or piloting, should operate according to guidelines rather than personal opinions. On the other hand, the laboratory staff believed they should only work in proportion to their salary, without necessarily adhering to all guidelines. In this context, what should the role of a true leader be? It was a challenging situation for me. Today, I can confidently say that my stance was correct, but back then, I was filled with uncertainty: "Am I being too strict for no reason?"

A Quiet, Yet Decisive Farewell

Perhaps you're wondering how I endured such difficult and ambiguous circumstances. My answer is simple: deeply rooted values. I was filled with a love for serving people, and the only thing that encouraged me to go on was the satisfied smiles of patients. I was committed to my word and deliberate in my decisions. However, just like most people born in May, I was patient, but once I realized that the environment was not suitable for me, I decided to leave.

At a laboratory improvement congress, the manager of a rival laboratory offered me an exciting opportunity, and my boss saw us talking. The next day, he asked me what we had discussed. I told him I was seriously considering leaving the organization. A few days later, he proposed a partnership and offered me some shares. Initially, I felt positive and thought my hardships had finally paid off, but given my knowledge of him, I didn't fully believe him. I was offered a negligible share, without notarization or a contract. I remained patient, but the increased responsibilities without sufficient support had put a lot of pressure on me.

In a meeting held at 7 PM on Wednesday, August 14, 2013,

which went on for three hours, a statement from my boss brought everything to an end:

"You haven't done anything here; this place has grown because of management and the shareholders' reputation!"

Perhaps he was right. I went to the laboratory the next morning, reported the test results, packed my belongings, and returned home. I never went back to that laboratory and never saw him again. However, I hope he has reconsidered his management style.

In Search of Answers

I walked away from the organization, left with nothing but my dreams and a series of unanswered questions:

- Who is a good manager?
- What qualities should a middle manager possess?
- What are standards, and how should they be implemented?

To find answers to my questions, I visited and collaborated with various laboratories in Tehran and attended international courses on "Quality Management Systems in the Laboratory". To my surprise, I realized that what I had been doing intuitively was in accordance with the standards; I simply hadn't known the item numbers! From how to interact with patients to how to issue test results, I had acted correctly. However, one point I didn't know was this: laboratory employees are also organizational clients, and paying attention to their emotions, needs, and motivation is part of the standards. I also successfully completed a course for executive managers of healthcare centers. I became familiar with organizational concepts, team building, the difference between a team and a group, and the principles of human resource management. Yet, the main question remained unanswered in my mind: How do I implement these principles?

A Rebirth

It was here that I became acquainted with the concept of coaching. I believe that if you are honest with yourself, God and the universe will show you the way, so I searched for a good mentor. In 2022, on Instagram, I saw a video by Dr. Shahab Anari about the purpose of life. It was as if a key turned in the locked door of my mind. I enrolled in North Star Coaching and Training Academy to become a professional coach.

In February 2025, a new Shahrzad was born. In the professional coach training course, I found the answers to all my questions and learned how to implement my knowledge. Following the completion of my program, I actively sought opportunities to realize my vision. During a professional event, I was introduced to an individual with a doctorate in business and a strong background as an international mentor. This meeting inspired me to take strategic steps toward fostering a coaching culture within healthcare organizations, with a particular focus on the laboratory sector. I developed proposals for several major institutions, and a laboratory located in Northern Tehran was the first to respond positively.

Shared Vision, Shared Expression

The technical manager of this center, Dr. Yaghoubi, shared a perspective very similar to mine. He was one of the only people I knew who recognized the similarities between a laboratory and the aviation industry, where both employees and clients are among the most valuable human assets. Both fields require high precision, flawless team coordination, and adherence to strict protocols to ensure safety and quality; even the slightest error can have serious consequences. However, laboratories face additional human challenges, such as direct interaction with patients and managing their emotions and anxiety, which distinguishes them from the aviation industry.

Dr. Yaghoubi, by studying fields beyond his medical specialization, planned to attract and retain qualified personnel and develop his team's capabilities. During an interview I had with him about leadership and establishing a coaching culture, I discovered many common and inspiring points. He believed that a true leader is someone who is a fighter yet humble, attributes success to their team, embraces challenges, works collaboratively, and strives to create achievements.

Successful leaders have grand human dreams and seek to address the needs of humanity today and tomorrow. They have deep respect for their subordinates. We believe that:

- The leader must define the organization's values and goals.
- Global transformations, whether opportunities or threats, should not derail the organization from its path.

- Motivating the team is one of the most important responsibilities of leadership.

Coaching: The Key to Effective Leadership in Healthcare and Laboratories

We believe that an effective leader, especially in healthcare and laboratories, must possess strong coaching skills. In this field, the client—whether an employee or a patient—plays a crucial role in the organization's success.

In a laboratory, similar to the aviation industry, clients are often anxious and concerned about their health. They require services that extend beyond technical equipment, encompassing respect, empathy, and human kindness—qualities that can only be provided by individuals who deeply understand the client's situation.

Conversely, the final product—laboratory test results—must be produced precisely according to established standards and guidelines. These requirements can create a sterile work environment. It is here that we fully appreciate the depth of Peter Drucker's insights into the complexities of healthcare, hospitals, and laboratories. Peter Drucker, in one of his lectures in Iran, said: "Hospitals are among the most complex organizations in human history and are extremely difficult to manage." Research conducted in our country[1] indicates that employees utilize only 11% of their true potential in the

---

1. Khodayari Shoti, N. (2021). Iran: Resource management, national capital and its impact on the socio-economic status of people. IOSR Journal of Humanities and Social Science, 26.

workplace. Why is this the case?

Coaching is a powerful method for leadership that empowers employees and narrows the gap between their potential capacity and efficiency. Motivated employees represent the organization's most significant competitive advantage. In a coaching culture, the leader is part of the team—not a distant authority figure. This environment encourages team members to raise problems without fear, fostering trust and open dialogue. Challenges are reframed as opportunities for growth rather than setbacks. Lessons learned are transformed into new processes, contributing to organizational knowledge management and supporting development at every level.

Coaching can transform an ordinary individual into a hardworking and inspiring team member. How? By truly listening to employees' demands, criticisms, and opinions, and valuing their input. In such an organization, there is no trace of informal, unhealthy, or toxic structures; tensions give way to growth-oriented challenges; the group evolves into a "team"; and it is this team that brings the organization closer to its goals.

While a directive management style may yield short-term results, sustainable progress requires principled leadership rooted in trust and shared responsibility. In organizations where a coaching culture is absent, managers frequently struggle to fully harness the talents and potential of their teams. Consequently, tensions arise among team members, leading to drained energy and project failures.

Coaching: Human-Centred Transformation in the Healthcare System

Coaching offers an opportunity for introspection, allowing individuals to reflect on their inner world, understand it without judgment, learn from it, and plan for the future. This path is unique for everyone, and coaching offers a safe and supportive space for discovery and acceptance. Reflecting on my life and career, I realize that coaching is not just a personal growth tool for me but an effective approach for creating transformation at deeper levels, particularly within the healthcare system and scientific laboratory environments. In settings driven by data, precision, and guidelines, coaching introduces a human dimension: conscious presence, internal reflection, and empowerment for effective decision-making. This approach enables professionals to respond with greater flexibility and clarity when navigating changes, challenges, and emotions.

With my experience at the intersection of science and personal development, I firmly believe that integrating coaching into the healthcare system and research structures is not merely a conscious choice but a necessity for a more sustainable and humane future. Coaching can foster an environment of psychological safety, ethical leadership, and meaningful communication, marking the beginning of a transformation that will enhance not only our professional performance but also the quality of our care and our human relationships. This change is perhaps more essential to humanity today than ever before.

Coaching as a New Approach to Management in Healthcare Centers

About the Author

Shahrzad Fakhri is a leading expert in enhancing healthcare service quality and organizational development in laboratories. She is the founder of Vista Quality Education and Development Company, an institution dedicated to helping new and medium-sized laboratories achieve sustainable growth by establishing quality management systems based on international standards such as ISO 15189 and ISO 9001.

In addition to implementing these systems, Shahrzad, as an organizational coach with an innovative approach, focuses on building cohesive teams, replacing traditional management models with effective leadership, and fostering a coaching-based organizational culture in healthcare centers and laboratories. She places special emphasis on the role of human resources as a key factor in service quality and customer satisfaction.

With over 25 years of professional experience in laboratory sciences, Shahrzad has held supervisory roles and served as the head of specialized departments in clinical, pathobiology, and genetics laboratories in Tehran. These experiences have provided her with a deep understanding of internal organizational challenges and the actual needs of healthcare centers.

Shahrzad's educational and specialized background includes:

- Bachelor of Laboratory Sciences from Jundishapur University of Medical Sciences, Ahvaz
- Master of Genetics from Azad University of Medical Sciences, Tehran
- Executive Management for Healthcare Centers (Health Care MBA) course from Jahad Daneshgahi, Shahid Beheshti University
- ISO 15189 Auditor and Lead Auditor course from AKS, the official representative of ASCB (Accreditation Service for Certifying Bodies), UK
- Certified Professional Coach from North Star Academy in Canada under the supervision of Dr. Shahab Anari (accredited by the International Coaching Federation)

Shahrzad firmly believes that nothing remains sustainable

without personal and team growth. She asserts that true quality arises from respect for people, continuous training, and conscious leadership. Her challenging experiences have inspired her professional journey, enabling her to reinvent herself through learning and now to assist others in overcoming their challenges.

Contact the author:

✉ enso.fakhr.coach@gmail.com
✉ sh.fakhr021@gmail.com
⦿ Enso.coachiing
◁ Enso Coaching
in shahrzad-fakhri
☏ +98 991 230 5132 and +98 912 345 9279

Seeking The Truth
A Journey Toward Self-Awareness, Transformation, and Self-Discovery

Dr. Roya Geravand

Seeking The Truth
A Journey Toward Self-Awareness, Transformation, and Self-Discovery

Dr. Roya Geravand
Coach, Project Manager and Business Analyst

Change will not come if we wait for someone else or for a better time. We are the ones we've been waiting for. We are the change that we seek.[1]

A Journey into the Unknown

Imagine you are walking in a foggy forest. The shadows of tall trees, the crunching whisper of dry leaves underfoot, and the mysterious sound of the wind through the branches immerse you in a vast unknown. At times, your heart races with fear; at other moments, curiosity sparks in your eyes. This forest mirrors the path of life: a place where you lose your way repeatedly, only to ultimately discover yourself.

Have you ever wondered why, despite all your efforts, something inside you feels hollow? Why, amid your numerous achievements and constant successes, do you feel that something is still missing? You are not alone. Many of us have reached such a point. This is where the alarms start to go off, signaling that a change and transformation must be made—one that begins deep within and transforms you into a

---
1. Obama, B. (2008, February 5). *[Speech transcript]*. Chicago, IL, United States.

stronger, more aware, and freer version of yourself.

The main issue is that many of us postpone change until the last moment, until we are forced to, when we have hit rock bottom. We wait until life stops us with unexpected shocks or until a deep pain grips our hearts and souls. But why should we wait for these wake-up calls? Why not consciously choose to change?

What if you wake up one day and realize you have been alive but not truly living for years? Life is about experience, change, growth, and rebirth amidst darkness. For this transformation, you must be brave enough to step into the unknown and wade through mysterious, unfamiliar swamps. There will be moments of doubt and suffering, but these moments promise that no matter where you are—whether at the peak of success or in despair—you still have the chance to change and embark on this incredible journey. You enjoy the greatest blessing of all: the gift of breath, and you are alive.

This chapter teaches you the signs of embarking on an inner journey, the necessity of it, and the means required to navigate its winding path. It reassures you that you are not, and will not be, the only one setting out on this journey, or in the middle or end of it; all of us, sooner or later, with varying degrees of pain, are compelled to embark on a journey, inner transformation, growth, and maturity.

The Inner Hidden Secret

In the heart of remote mountains, amongst vast plains and lush forests, lived a delicate, agile, and majestic creature known as the Musk deer. It possessed a magical scent, a pleasant fragrance that flowed in the breeze and filled the nostrils of every passerby. However, the deer itself was unaware of this secret and did not know where the fragrance originated.

Every time a gentle wind blew and spread the delightful scent in the air, the Musk deer, captivated by this unique aroma, would set out to find its source. In search of this enchanting fragrance, it spent many long days and nights wandering; it traversed valleys, climbed mountains, roamed forests, visited flower gardens, and searched near mountain springs. Yet, every time it drew near to the destination, the scent seemed to drift further away.

Then one day, after years of futile searching, at the peak of despair, when it could no longer had the vigor to continue, it collapsed in the grass from sheer disappointment and fatigue. For the first time, it relinquished the fight and the chase, staring at the blue sky and the vast world around it. Just then, a wind blew, and the scent of musk filled the air. Suddenly, the deer realized the truth for the first time: what it had been seeking all these years was hidden within itself.

> Nothing in this world lies outside of you.
> Whatever you seek, look within—it's you.[1]

---

1. Rumi, Divan-e Shams

Signs of Embarking on a Journey and the Need for Transformation

There are moments in life when we seem to be suspended in a limbo of doubt and aimlessness. We feel that something is missing within us, but we don't know what it is. We explore countless paths, searching for something invisible yet powerful. However, the more we struggle, the more lost and purposeless we feel. How long will this search continue? Should we wait for life to awaken us with a harsh blow? Or can we consciously choose the path of transformation?

Many subtle yet profound signs in our daily lives indicate that our current path no longer satisfies our soul. Some of the most significant of these signs include:

1. **Feeling Empty and Aimless:** If nothing in life makes your heartbeat faster and excites you, perhaps it's time to pause and reassess your path. This sense of emptiness is not exclusive to those who have failed or given up; it often appears in the lives of individuals who, on the surface, seem highly successful but feel disconnected deep down. This feeling can be one of life's most powerful turning points, offering a chance for deep and meaningful change, provided we are ready to embrace it and turn it into an opportunity.

2. **Repeating Similar Mistakes:** Have you been trapped in cycles and similar situations that yield disappointing results? The repetition of such

patterns signals deep-rooted limiting beliefs in your subconscious and highlights the fundamental need to change them.[1] Many of us are stuck in a closed loop of repetition, waking up each day with the same old thoughts, feelings, and habits. Meanwhile, a soft voice within us whispers that something is missing and needs to change. However, we often ignore this voice, as breaking old habits feels like shattering a hard and dark cocoon. Yet, isn't the beauty of a butterfly the result of breaking free from the cocoon that once held it captive?

3. **Feeling Trapped and Deeply Unfulfilled:** Sometimes it feels like you're stuck inside an invisible cage, as if there's no way out and no clear path forward. You've hit a dead end, facing a glass ceiling that feels unbreakable, and it seems like there's no room left to grow or move ahead. But what you may not realize is this: the master key to your freedom is already in your hands.

4. **Fear of the Future and Lack of Meaning[2] in Life:** Does the future feel overwhelmingly uncertain and frightening? Do you suffer from anxiety, confusion, and bewilderment? Such feelings may stem from the fact that, deep inside, you know that the path you're

---

1. Jung, C. G. (1959). *Aion: Researches into the Phenomenology of the Self.* Princeton University Press
2. Frankl, V. E. (2006). *Man's Search for Meaning.* Beacon Press. (Originally published in 1946)

on is leading nowhere. Perhaps the foundations of your life were built on shaky or misplaced ground from the beginning. Whatever the reason, your mind feels like a tangled ball of thoughts, draining more and more of your mental energy each day.

5. **Depression and Chronic Fatigue:** When your body and mind constantly feel worn out, it means you are enduring something incompatible with your soul and the deeper layers of your psyche. This alarm warns you of the conflict and cognitive dissonance[1] in your soul, life, and behavior that have been concealed for years, but its ominous shadow continues to feed on your pure energy.

The Urge for Transformation: Why Should We Change?

If you stare at the calm surface of a pond, you will see a reflection of yourself. But throw a stone into the water, and the image changes; waves appear, and the once-calm surface becomes turbulent. This is what change and transformation signify in our lives: a movement in the depths of existence, breaking the silence, and heralding a rebirth.

Change is the inevitable law of life. Just as the beautiful nature transforms through the four seasons, we, too, must allow the seasons of our lives to evolve. The world is constantly

---

1. Festinger, L. (1957). *A theory of Cognitive Dissonance.* Stanford University Press.

changing and transforming, but we often resist and fear change, unlike nature. Why? Change involves crossing into the unknown. We become accustomed to our daily lives and habits that, though unsatisfying, are at least familiar. Breaking these patterns, leaving our comfort zones, and embracing uncertainty can feel daunting. But isn't every blossom born from profound change?

If we resist change and cling to our past, we will stagnate, leading to endless suffering. What is the first step toward change? Self-awareness: a deep understanding of ourselves, our beliefs, our emotions, and what has limited us from experiencing a life of authenticity and light.

Self-Awareness: The Key to Self-Discovery and Change

The musk deer spent years searching for a scent that came from itself; this reflects a situation we often find ourselves in. Until we cultivate self-awareness, we may not realize that the source of most feelings and problems lies hidden within us.

Self-awareness involves looking inward and recognizing wounds, fears, dreams, and abilities that we may have previously overlooked. Without self-awareness, any change will be superficial, as we will remain unaware of what needs to change.[1]

---

1. Rogers, C. (1961). *On Becoming a Person: A Therapist's View of Psychotherapy*. Houghton Mifflin.

> He who knows and longs to know still more,
> Will lift himself to fortune's highest shore.
> He who knows but does not know he knows,
> Holds a full cup, yet thirsting ever goes.
> He who knows not, yet yearns to understand,
> Shall free his soul and mind from folly's hand.[1]

Self-awareness encompasses various components and dimensions: physical self-awareness, psychological self-awareness, spiritual self-awareness, and social self-awareness.

The **'Johari Window'** model[2] is a powerful tool on the path to self-awareness, also known as the feedback/disclosure self-awareness model. Introduced in 1955 by psychologists Joseph Luft and Harry Ingham, this model consists of four main areas:

1. **Open Area:** What both we and others know about us, including our interests, desires, personality traits, skills, and behaviors that are clear to everyone.

2. **Blind Area:** Characteristics that others observe in us but of which we are unaware. This aspect of our existence can only be discovered through feedback from others. In this area, the role of a coach as a benevolent and non-judgmental person can be particularly effective.

3. **Hidden Area:** Parts of our existence that we know

---
1. Mulla Ahmad Naraghi
2. Luft, J.; Ingham, H. (1955). *The Johari window, a graphic model of interpersonal awareness*. Proceedings of the western training laboratory in group development. Los Angeles: University of California, Los Angeles.

but conceal from others, such as fears, dreams, and suppressed emotions. As understanding and trust develop between us and those around us, we can share information about ourselves through self-disclosure.

4. **Unknown Area:** Aspects that neither we nor others are aware of. This realm contains talents, mental limitations, conditioning, weaknesses, and potentials that can only be uncovered through a deep inner journey. As an individual becomes more self-aware, the extent of this unknown area decreases and is integrated into the open area. The coaching process, through powerful questions and thoughtful reflection, can help uncover answers and root causes of issues, moving beyond superficial layers.

The more aware we become of these four areas, the deeper our inner journey becomes, and our connection with ourselves and others becomes clearer and more transparent.

Coaching and Self-Coaching: A Way to Navigate Through the Fog of Life

Coaching[1] is an art that accompanies individuals on their path of transformation and change. A professional coach uses their skills and competencies to help clients emerge from confusion and chaos, achieving order and clarity. However, it is the

---

1. Elias, S. (2012). *Coaching: A Path to Personal Transformation.* New York: Insight Publications.

individual who must take the initiative and act.

What if we don't have a coach? This is where self-coaching[1] comes into play. It means being your own coach. But how?

- **Asking Robust Questions:**
  - What in my life needs to change?
  - Which of my beliefs are holding me back from progressing?
  - If there were no fear or limitations, what path would I choose?
- **Getting Feedback from Others:** Generally, we do not see our blind spots. Feedback from trusted individuals can provide us with a better image of ourselves. We can sometimes be like an eye that can observe others but is unable to see itself.

Hear this truth from me, pure and whole:
It is your closeness to the world that has distanced you from your soul.[2]

- **Observing and Recording Thoughts, Feelings and Behaviors:** Keeping a notebook to record daily thoughts, emotions, and reactions can gradually reveal our inefficient mental patterns[3].
- **Practicing Being in the Moment:** Mindfulness is a

---

1. Fischer, J. (2017). *Self-Coaching and Mental Strength: Techniques for Personal Change.* London: Mind Path Press.
2. Shaikh Mahmoud Shabestari
3. Beck, A. T. (1976). *Cognitive Therapy and Emotional Disorders.* New York: International Universities Press.

powerful tool for enhancing self-awareness.[1] If we pause for a moment and introspect, we may realize that the answers to all our questions lie in the silence within.

How to Change?

Change is not a sudden leap and will not happen overnight. It is a journey that must be taken step by step. However, if we know how to navigate this path of transformation, we can experience less pain throughout the process of change and transformation and become the best version of ourselves.[2]

Much travel is needed for the unripe soul to mature[3]

Here are some fundamental solutions to begin this journey and stay committed to it:

1. **Enhancing Self-Awareness:** Before any transformation, you must first understand what within you truly needs to shift and what your main issue is.

2. **Fully Accepting Responsibility for Your Life:** Your life is the result of your choices. If you don't like your current situation, you must change it yourself. Part of life happens to us, but we should not shrug off the part that we are responsible for changing and play the role of a victim, defeated and desperate.

---

1. Kabat-Zinn, J. (1994). *Wherever you go, there you are: Mindfulness meditation in everyday life*. Hyperion.
2. Maslow, A.H. (1954). *Motivation and Personality*. New York: Harper & Row.
3. Sa'di

3. **Exiting the Comfort Zone:** No growth happens in comfort. You have to step on a path that challenges you. As long as you stay in old frameworks, no growth happens. Transformation requires abandoning old, rotten habits.

4. **Being Open to Failure:** Failures are valuable lessons. Don't fear them; instead, use them as a launching pad and a ladder for progress. Failure is part of the growth journey, not a sign of the end.

5. **Facing Fears:** Facing your fears is where you feel the most trepidation; it is also where the greatest growth awaits you.

6. **Utilizing Coaches and Guides:** Sometimes, we need someone to guide us on the path to transformation. Coaches, psychologists, and spiritual guides can accompany you on this journey. Self-awareness, introspection, and self-coaching also help you navigate this path. One can gradually progress through growth by acquiring knowledge and skills, and learning through action, practice, and continuous repetition.

7. **Turning Change into a Habit:** Take a small step every day and strive to be a little better than yesterday. Significant changes begin with small daily habits.

Return to the Source: Where the Light Begins

Transformation is often accompanied by pain, but the pain of awareness is a sacred suffering that is infinitely more rewarding than the agony of remaining in ignorance and incapacity. Embarking on an inner journey and the path of change requires strong determination and can mark the beginning of a new chapter in your life. It is the starting point of profound transformation—a journey in which you free yourself from both visible and invisible chains of the past, discard false masks, and choose a new path with love and respect for yourself. This path can lead to the salvation of your inner and outer life, allowing you to experience inner peace, liberation, love, human dignity, and the glory of existence, or even become a guide for others on this winding journey.

Like the musk deer, after a strenuous journey, we will realize that the lost scent of pure musk has always originated from within us. Everything we seek—peace, happiness, love, respect, and value—has been hidden within us from the very beginning.

> For years, our hearts have desired the Cup of Jamshid[1],
> Yearning for what they already possess.[2]

In the journey of transformation, there comes a moment when

---

1. *The Cup of Jamshid (Jam-e Jam)* is a legendary cup in Persian mythology linked to the ancient king Jamshid. It was said to contain an elixir of immortality and was used for divination, revealing truths about the world and the future. In Persian literature, it symbolizes ultimate wisdom and insight.
2. Hafez

you are no longer the silkworm, and not yet the butterfly. You are no longer who you once were, and not yet the new self you are becoming. It is like a spaceship that has lifted off from the familiar terrain of your former being, and is now floating into the vast unknown of your becoming, toward a destination. The length of this journey may at times leave you frustrated, discouraged, or disheartened; you may feel lost in darkness or enveloped in a haze of uncertainty that makes the path ahead unclear. Yet with every step you take toward self-awareness and discovery of your inner truth, the flame within you burns brighter, drawing you one step closer to becoming that butterfly—a beautiful, free and, liberated. It is the persistence along the path that will ultimately carry you to your destination, where you are truly meant to be.

Seeking The Truth

A Journey Toward Self-Awareness, Transformation, and Self-Discovery

About the Author

Dr. Roya Geravand is a coach, project manager and business analyst with over 18 years of experience in large-scale oil and gas projects. She combines a unique blend of technical expertise, managerial insight, and human understanding throughout her professional journey. Dr. Geravand holds international PMP®[1] and PMI-PBA®[2] certifications from the Project Management Institute (PMI) in the United States.

In 2007, Roya joined Pars Oil and Gas Company through the Elites Program, which is responsible for developing the

---

1. Project Management Professional (PMP)
2. PMI Professional in Business Analysis (PMI-PBA)

South Pars gas field[1] as well as several other strategic fields. She earned her Ph.D. in Petroleum Engineering (Reservoirs) from the University of Tehran, and conducted part of her dissertation research at Universiti Teknologi Petronas (UTP), as a visiting doctoral scholar. Additionally, she has completed a Doctor of Business Administration (DBA) program at the University of Tehran, and has published numerous scientific articles in national and international journals and conferences.

A significant turning point in Roya's life was embarking on the path of self-discovery, transformation, coaching, and self-coaching. Her interest in psychotherapeutic approaches and psychological sciences, combined with her professional training, scientific studies and personal experiences, has transformed her into a profound and self-made individual. She is now equipped to inspire, accompany, and guide others on their paths to transformation and growth.

What sets Roya apart is her distinctive integration of specialized knowledge, leadership, managerial skills, and a humanistic approach to personal and organizational development. She helps individuals, managers, and organizations in moving beyond mere survival and stepping into a state of true flourishing.

Fluent in English and French, in addition to her first language, Persian, Roya leverages her language skills to establish

---

1. The "*South Pars*" gas field, known as the "*North Dome*" in Qatar, is the world's largest natural gas field. It is located on the shared border between Iran and Qatar in the Persian Gulf.

effective and professional communication at the international level.

Ways to contact the author:

in Roya Geravand (PhD, DBA, PMP®, PMI-PBA®)
✉ drroyageravand@gmail.com

No More Waiting

A Narrative of Change, Self-Awareness, and the Power of Choice through Coaching

Dennis Gharibian

No More Waiting
A Narrative of Change, Self-Awareness, and the Power of Choice through Coaching

Dennis Gharibian

System Designer, Entrepreneur, and Certified Life Coach

> If you're an actual wayfarer, you must walk through blood,
> Headlong you'll fall—still rise, still trudge through mud.
> Set foot upon the path—ask not where it may go;
> The road itself will tell you what you need to know.[1]

Life has shown me many times that no matter how strong I am, it will still knock me down, but I am not one to stay down. Today, in retrospect, I feel that every failure, every fall, and every wrong path I have taken have transformed me into who I am today. My life journey has been full of challenges and ups and downs. Just when I thought I had planned for the future—having completed my military service, become a consulting engineer, and progressed to the head of a technical office—I suddenly faced my first major life challenge. At that time, my life had a strong pillar: my father!

Lessons I Learned from My Father

My father was four years old when he lost his father. His

---
1. Poem by Attar Neyshaboori, a Persian Sufi poet and mystic known for his profound exploration of the spiritual path and the inner journey of the soul.

mother raised him by working in other people's homes. Despite all the hardships and financial struggles, he managed to finish school. He earned a diploma in accounting and began his career. After getting married, he built a stable life and transitioned into a career in project management.

My father was a quiet but thoughtful man who always prioritized others. He was always ready to help others wholeheartedly. Through his behavior and words, he taught my sister and me countless life lessons and held a special place in our lives. Although he might not have had much wealth, he possessed a wealthy mindset and attitude. He was graceful in character and demeanor, and he constantly supported me on my path of learning and growth. My father was my guide, passing down so many lessons and life experiences to me. He was the rock of our family.

Just when I thought life would continue as it always had, that dreadful day arrived. I lost the hand I thought would hold mine forever, and with it, the person I believed I could rely on for the rest of my life. That day, I learned a precious lesson: "Nothing in this world is permanent, and in the blink of an eye, everything can change." Life can lift someone from poverty to royalty and bring someone else from royalty to poverty. I went from having a perfect father to becoming fatherless. That's when I truly understood what he meant when he used to tell me that maturity isn't about age. I grew up overnight! The night before, I was a pampered little boy; the next morning, I was the man of the house!

When a foundational element of your life suddenly disappears, the world becomes dark, gloomy, and unfamiliar. However, hidden within that instability are lessons no school could ever teach. As painful as loss is, it can mark the beginning of growth. That bitter experience was perhaps the moment I was born on the inside, with a new perspective, a deeper understanding of my father, life, and what it truly means to grow up.

A Plan for a Dream

Losing this precious treasure transformed the path of my life. I found myself in a place I never expected. Enduring this great shock was even harder for my sister. Now, in addition to carrying the heavy sorrow of losing my father, I was also helping my sister not to abandon her studies and providing support for my mother. When my situation somewhat stabilized, I made a big decision: I needed a new beginning for survival and growth. I had to answer a crucial question: Who do I want to be? I decided to immigrate, ready to face whatever awaited me. I took on every job I could find, steadily building my experience until, after two years, I found stability. I obtained several certificates and entered a new phase of life: engineering in a new country. I progressed on this path and eventually became a manager, even serving as the supervisor of my group for a time. This achievement marked a significant milestone compared to where I started. The internet became a vast world and a launching platform for me; I felt that with its help, I could connect with many people. The profits and losses of this market, along with its fluctuations, taught me invaluable lessons.

Immigration is not merely a physical displacement; it often involves moving away from a past filled with pain, dependency, and despair toward an uncertain future brimming with opportunities. In moments when the ground shakes beneath our feet, a voice within us suddenly asks: "Who do you want to be?" This simple question can serve as a turning point for a new beginning. On the journey of immigration and self-rebuilding, sometimes the only capital we possess is the "memory" of those no longer here and the "belief" in our abilities.

The Turning Point of My Life

A new phase in my life began when I got married, and the birth of my son set me on a fresh path. At this stage, I felt my son was the fruit of my life, and I needed to nurture him. However, his unexpected illness swept through our lives like a storm, draining our focus and energy. The hardships of this period transformed me; I learned compassion, became more patient, and experienced profound distress. I won't go into details, but this time taught me that sometimes you must endure and give yourself time to heal. As my son's health improved, and with the unconditional support and companionship of my spouse, I decided to embark on a new path. With his recovery, I began an inner journey that I now call inner coaching—a path marked by deep contemplation, new goals, and a conscious commitment to personal growth.

During my child's illness, we faced days when mental, emotional, and physical pressures were exhausting. Today, when I look back at those days, I believe the crisis was a turning point in forming a new version of myself. On the path of rebirth, I gained a deeper understanding of myself; I discovered abilities I never knew I had and identified limiting beliefs that had held me back. I came to a new understanding of fears that had silently hindered my progress: fear of failure, fear of success, and, most importantly, fear of trusting myself. I would tell myself, "What if I fail again? If I succeed, do I deserve it?" These inner dialogues taught me that often it is not the problem itself, but our hesitation in decision-making, rooted in those limiting beliefs, that prevents us from growing. At this point in my life, I accepted that I had to change, just like a patient who initially denies and then accepts their condition; this acceptance is the first step in the healing process. I learned that I must confront all my fears and doubts. This was the starting point for realizing my long-held dream: helping others.

Supporting my sister in her studies and accompanying patients during my child's illness revealed my heartfelt desire: to make an impact and have a job I love. Once, in a counseling session, I told one of my clients, "Choose a job that you do not do solely for the salary, but for inner satisfaction. If you take a job you don't like, you may earn a decent income, but you will spend it trying to fill the voids in your life. However, if you have a job you love, that love will fill the voids in your existence, and you will feel you are in the right place."

When Standing Up Is a Fresh Start

To achieve my long-held dream, I began learning skills that would guide me toward my main goal. I focused on communication, marketing, and sales while trying to generate some income and gain knowledge. Along the way, I had the opportunity to meet renowned figures like Brian Tracy, Tony Robbins, and Dean Graziosi. I learned valuable lessons about positive thinking, harnessing inner power, and goal-setting, and I'm grateful to share these insights with others.

Sometimes, the crises that knock us down become the very opportunities that rebuild us. The pains we experience can transform into seeds of awareness, as long as we confront them and seek meaning in our struggles. Engaging in inner dialogue with our fears, doubts, and limiting beliefs may be challenging, but it marks the beginning of liberation. The moment you ask yourself, "Who am I really, and who do I want to become?" is when true growth begins.

The Beginning of a Change

A turning point in my learning journey was getting acquainted with Dr. Shahab Anari. Knowing him initiated a new phase in my life, propelling me into a stage I had passionately pursued for years but couldn't describe in words. The ups and downs of life taught me that change is constant, yet we sometimes need guidance, knowledge, and the right tools to embrace it. When I first encountered the concept of coaching, it felt like I had opened a door to a new world. Coaching is not merely a skill; it is a fresh approach to understanding oneself, others, and life itself.

For me, coaching is not just a profession but an opportunity to assign meaning to experiences and turn pain into awareness. I began studying this discipline with great enthusiasm, recognizing that it would undeniably impact my personal and professional growth. Initially, coaching seemed like a set of techniques, but as I moved forward, I realized it is an inner journey where I must confront my limiting beliefs and reshape my mental patterns. I learned to pave the way for success by creating a clear vision for my life. These insights led to positive changes in both my personal and professional spheres. By attending various training courses and participating in practical workshops, I strengthened my coaching skills and shared this knowledge with others. Now, I am wholeheartedly pursuing this path with indescribable enthusiasm, eager to inspire those on similar journeys. I have participated in numerous projects aimed at helping individuals better understand themselves, overcome internal obstacles, and achieve their goals. Each time I witnessed someone discovering a new path in their life through coaching, my motivation to continue grew stronger. A significant aspect of this journey was witnessing profound transformations in different individuals; some uncovered hidden talents for the first time, others learned to leave behind their mental barriers, and others gained the confidence to move toward their goals. Seeing these transformations brought me deep satisfaction and joy.

Change is not always easy or quick. Sometimes, even the most challenging moments carry the most fruitful transformations. But what makes change possible is not just will, but rather acceptance, awareness, and the ability to adapt to it, and for this, change must become a part of life. Coaching was a change for me that became a part of my lifestyle; a style based on awareness, growth, and helping others. It not only helped me become a better person but also enabled me to make an impact on others' lives. I have always wanted to help those around me and extend a hand of friendship toward them, but I lacked the necessary knowledge, experience, and skills. After becoming familiar with coaching, I acquired the professional skills, knowledge, and expertise required to help others, continually expanding my knowledge through the collection and study of books.

Life Cannot Be Left to Fate

Coaching changed the course of my life. Through my inner journey, I realized that I should not remain passive and wait for the right moment. Coaching taught me that by believing in our inner abilities, we can identify possible paths and, with the power of choice, take steps in the desired direction. It not only enhances self-awareness but also helps us recognize the requirements of the first step, enabling us to take small but continuous actions to traverse even the longest roads.

I want to share these learnings with all those who are still waiting—those who need to know that the control of the ship of fate is in their own hands. I waited long years for better conditions, an ideal job position, and a more comfortable life, but that moment never arrived. As Brian Tracy states, "Many of us are standing on a certain street waiting to get on a bus, oblivious to the fact that no bus will ever pass that street!" To reach our goals, we need to create the right path.[1]

Coaching was a powerful tool for me that allowed me to help hundreds of people change their lives. Every person has dreams that may initially seem out of reach, but with effort, perseverance, and self-belief, they can be realized. I had a dream, too: writing and working in the field of coaching. Today, I proudly say that I have taken steps toward my dreams, though it was not easy. Many still believe that fate is predetermined and that we should wait to see what happens, but the truth is that no one is going to change our lives except ourselves. Learning—whether through books, podcasts, or training courses—becomes meaningful when it leads to action. Many have learned but never acted. Knowledge that does not lead to action is a mental burden that hinders our progress. Looking at the world's successful brands, we see that behind every success was an individual who, despite

---

1. 500 inspirational & motivational quotes by Brian Tracy by" Saeed Sikiru: https://www.scribd.com/document/668303960/Brian-Tracy-Quotes-500-Inspirational-and-Motivational-Quotes-Brian-Tracy. Accessed on June 5, 2025.

expectations, forged their own path, made mistakes, fell, and stood up again. They did not wait for a magical opportunity but learned from the journey with each misstep.

Let's not wait. Others do not create our future; we shape our own destiny with our choices, decisions, and actions. If you have a dream, take a step—however small—right now. It doesn't matter how difficult the path is; what matters is starting. On this journey, there will be challenges, but every obstacle is an opportunity for growth and progress. If you have faith in your path, you will reach your destination. Today, I am not only taking steps toward my dreams but also sharing this message with you:

You are the hero of your own life. Build your life the way you want. Fate is in your hands; start today!

If you need guidance on the path of change, coaching can be your guiding light. It helps you consciously draw your life path with transparency, the power of choice, and the necessary knowledge.

No More Waiting

A Narrative of Change, Self-Awareness, and the Power of Choice through Coaching

About The Author

Dennis Gharibian is a purposeful coach, seasoned entrepreneur, and engineering professional with a clear mission: to empower individuals to transform their lives, elevate their mindset, and achieve authentic success in the digital age. With over 15 years of hands-on experience in business, coaching, and engineering, Dennis has positioned himself as a trusted guide for those ready to reach their full potential.

Born in Iran and now based in Los Angeles, Dennis blends global insight with real-world expertise. Upon moving to the United States in 2006, he brought with him not only his qualifications as a Civil Engineer and Electrical Low-Voltage

Designer but also a deep desire to impact lives. His journey into the world of online business began in 2008 through various marketing platforms, where he quickly recognized the power of digital freedom and personal branding.

However, Dennis's path to mastery was not without obstacles. His early ventures taught him that success requires not just tools but also complete and guided training, inner clarity, and relentless commitment. In 2022, after years of searching for the right model, he discovered a value-based digital business system that offered both personal growth and scalable professional development. This became the launchpad for his coaching and entrepreneurial renaissance.

Today, Dennis stands as a respected leader in the online business and coaching sphere, combining his technical background with deep emotional intelligence and spiritual alignment. As a certified coach operating under the ICF[1] Standards, he focuses on mindset development, life path design, self-discipline, and strategic goal-setting. His unique approach integrates high-performance coaching with modern marketing systems, enabling his clients to develop scalable, profitable, and goal-based businesses.

A passionate mentor and service-oriented leader, Dennis believes **that true success is measured not by what you achieve alone but by how many people you help along the way.** Whether he is leading training sessions, mentoring international clients, or creating impactful content across

---

1. International Coaching Federation

social media platforms, his mission remains the same: to awaken maturity in others and help them live a life of meaning, freedom, and impact.

Dennis is a father whom his son is proud of, a multilingual communicator (fluent in English, Persian, and Armenian), and a firm believer in faith, kindness, and perseverance. His mantra, "Be kind to each other," reflects his personal life and professional ethos.

Through his coaching programs, live sessions, and leadership training, Dennis invites individuals from all walks of life—professionals, creatives, parents, and aspiring entrepreneurs—to break free from limitations, rise with confidence, and step boldly into their highest potential.

You can contact him via:

- www.DennisGharibianCoaching.com
- Info@DennisGharibianCoaching.com
- Dennis Gharibian
- +1 (818) 464 6066, +1 (818) 649 4963

Whispers of the Soul

Gooya Ghiasi

Whispers of the Soul

Gooya Ghiasi

Life Purpose Coach

The wound is the place where the light enters you.[1]

The sunlight streamed through the large window behind me, reflecting off the mirror and transforming the thick cosmetology textbook in front of me into what seemed like a mysterious, coded map. Although reading was forbidden during hands-on training sessions, I would secretly sit behind the mirror and review the book because learning the language and earning certification in this field felt more urgent to me than practicing skills I had long mastered. Even the thought of taking an exam in an unfamiliar language made my heart race with anxiety.

That day, after finishing my practical work, I managed to steal a few moments to study. In the ordinary atmosphere of the class, everyone was absorbed in their routines— until that unexpected moment when the door opened, and two college administrators entered. Their faces were calm, but their eyes betrayed deep concern. A brief silence filled the room as all eyes turned to them. One of them spoke in a quiet but firm voice: "Due to the outbreak of the COVID-19 virus, classes are suspended. Please leave the campus immediately."

---

1. Rumi

The room erupted in murmurs. Students rushed to pack their belongings in their lockers, hoping for a brief interruption. But I immediately gathered my things and placed them in the car. A voice in my mind whispered, "This isn't temporary."

On the seemingly endless road ahead, dreadful thoughts refused to leave me. The strange illness was no longer a rumor; it was a deadly reality looming nearby. But this fear wasn't unfamiliar. I had tasted it before in the twists of fate. In a blink, the past unfolded before me.

Resilience

I was nineteen when I entered a traditional marriage, in a society that, because of my beliefs, denied me the chance to continue my education. The stark differences between our families gradually distanced me from my true self, burying me beneath layers of expectations that were never my own. Yet, I kept the image of that passionate dreamer inside me who longed to be an influential person in the world. Years later, in an effort to recover myself, achieve peace, and rebuild a sense of community, I chose to learn hairstyling. However, starting work in this profession was problematic, since, at that time, being a woman seeking independence was like walking through a silent battlefield.

Motherhood came quickly—before I'd had the chance to discover who I was, what I valued, or what I dreamed of becoming. I was overwhelmed by questions I didn't yet know how to ask, let alone answer. One day, I locked eyes with my young child, his gaze glowing with innocence and trust. A voice stirred deep within me: *"These questioning and hopeful eyes are my reason for my life. They will be the light in the darkness of the world."* So, despite all the difficulties, I devoted my heart to work and life. Step by step, with doubt and hope, I moved forward until on the verge of some balance, my life changed its course...

In October 2010, when registering my son at an English language institute, a colorful advertisement caught my eye: "U.S. Green Card Lottery." I had never heard of it. Curious, I asked my husband. He grinned and said, "Go for it! We've always been lucky." I filled out the form, unaware that sometimes simple choices could bring about the greatest changes. A few months later, in utter disbelief, we received a strange call —we had won the lottery. What began as a joke became one of the most serious challenges of my life. I, who had never even considered immigration, now had to choose: to stay in a land where I had deep roots, or to go to a country that might provide a more secure future for my children. Still reeling from the news, while coming down the last step of a store, I twisted my ankle so much so that I fainted on the spot from the pain. My right leg was dislocated and had to stay in a cast for four weeks. I wanted to scream—not realizing this pain was only the beginning to the sufferings I had ahead!

On a cloudy February night in 2010, while I was struggling with my cast, the doorbell rang. News of my husband's younger brother's sudden death struck like a thunderbolt.

Grief flooded our lives. It was as if fate wanted to teach us the sorrow of loss and farewell, all at once. In those days, I believed that leaving was not logical, and my husband should stay with his family. This thought somewhat calmed the chaos within me; because parting from my loved ones, from the scent of orange blossoms in the alleys of my Shiraz, was not easy. But my husband made a different decision. On June 20, 2011, my children and I set foot in a new land.

My parents and especially my brother—who had been living in California —had already laid a welcoming foundation for our arrival. Everything seemed in place and Perfect—except for me. Internally, I was lost in a storm of homesickness, isolation, alienation, confusion, and cultural shock. I also had to care for my children's emotional well-being, particularly my son, who was grieving the loss of his young uncle and friends just as he entered adolescence. To make matters worse, my husband had stayed behind in Iran for a while. Our limited communication only deepened my sense of loneliness. Meanwhile, I tried to be a source of strength for my aging parents as they navigated life in a foreign land. A voice inside me whispered, *"This place will never feel like home."*

Two months later, my husband joined us. By then, I was emotionally and physically drained. Alarmed by my condition, he decided to take us back to our homeland, Iran. The next two years were a struggle—emotionally, socially, and spiritually. I endured judgment and fought to reclaim peace only to face a painful reality.

On a sweltering July afternoon in 2014, I handed my husband's test results to the doctor. A horrifying truth, like a devastating blow, settled on my soul; a silent, creeping, and ruthless illness had taken root in my husband's body. I froze, as if everything had slipped entirely out of my control. Life was testing my strength; relentlessly and mercilessly.

A few days later, right on my birthday, I was standing behind the operating room door. As the doctor came out, I involuntarily ran toward him: "Was it malignant?"

"Yes! But fortunately, you realized it early." Although the doctor had said "fortunately," the path was not easy. How did those moments pass?! Only God knows.

In September 2015, I packed up for immigration once again. But this time, not by force, but with an informed decision and a firm will, hoping that in this new land, my children would unfurl their wings and embrace the freedom to chart their own paths in life.

After enduring the many challenges of immigration, I returned to hairstyling. But in the afternoon of the last Friday of May 2019, time seemed to pause on the verge of change, and the world, embroiled in a new crisis, stood on the edge of a terrifying precipice. A mysterious force, disguised as a tiny virus, was lying in wait to shatter the borders of our world and ruthlessly steal what we cherished. A voice echoed in my mind: *"Every time you're ready to take a new step, failure awaits."*

In the Embrace of Words

As a gentle breeze passed through my car window, the present took me back to life through the dust of memories. Reflecting on the past, I realized that life could never be fully controlled—and no external savior was coming. This bitter awareness brought me to a brilliant truth: In the end, it is only I—"Raha"—who must walk through the depths of my fears. I cannot master the unknowns of life, but I can learn how to manage my thoughts and feelings better. As Viktor Frankl said, "Everything can be taken from a man but one thing—the last of the human freedoms—to choose one's attitude in any given set of circumstances."

To get through this period, I needed a safe haven I knew well: my constant companion, the book. The love of reading had taken root in my soul from childhood; my father, a thoughtful man, continually encouraged me to learn and inquire, and my mother, with her nightly stories, planted the magic of words in my heart. The next day, I visited a nearby library, eager to search the shelves, but found nothing in my native language. Immigration had also robbed me of this deep connection. Although I attempted to engage with English books, I still found it difficult to connect with the unfamiliar words. I considered getting an e-reader, though it could never replace the feeling of the touch of real paper.

Finally, I found the book I had longed to read: *When Nietzsche Wept* by Irvin D. Yalom. I finished it in two days. Like a student discovering a favorite subject, I eagerly jotted down the book's dialogues in my notebook with childlike enthusiasm. For me, writing was more than just words—it was a tool for reflection and processing my feelings and thoughts. I had always turned to writing in difficult times, hoping that light would emerge from within.

Next, I read *Love in the Time of Cholera*, a tale of illness, death, love, and the agony of waiting. The flawed, complex characters searching for a meaningful connection with one another reminded me of ourselves, as if Márquez had foreseen, decades earlier, the viral fever of our own era—the emotional and physical isolation brought on by a pandemic that touched every life.

Then came *Man's Search for Meaning*. It was incredible, leading me into a profound exploration of my soul. I couldn't figure out when this simple yet profound word, *meaning*, first took root in me, but I knew that in the heart of many life twists, I had always been searching for a reason; an unconscious quest that, in the hard moments, was like a thread pulling me from the edge of despair. As Nietzsche describes the essence of this quest, "He who has a why to live can bear almost any how."

I read tirelessly. Reading wasn't an escape from fears—it was a path to my lost "self."

The Dawn

Over time, I realized that society—especially women in their influential roles as mothers—has a deep need for greater awareness, particularly in self-awareness and effective communication. This feeling had its roots in my valuable experiences in Shiraz; a place where I had become familiar with concepts such as personal growth and development in educational groups and alongside capable consultants. Also, years of working in the cosmetology profession and conversing with women from various layers of society had acquainted me with their world of emotions, desires, and needs.

These experiences, inspired by a television program called *Open book*, which introduced a practical book each week, planted the seeds of a new idea. On March 8, 2022—International Women's Day—I invited a few close friends to an intimate online gathering and shared my vision for a virtual book club. At first, only a handful joined, but little by little, our small circle blossomed into a lively and growing community. Our first read was *I'm OK, You're OK* by Thomas A. Harris, a book exploring transactional analysis.

Each book we read opened doors to meaningful conversations and guided me toward greater self-understanding and a stronger connection with others and the world. One day, a dear counselor made a thought-provoking suggestion: "Raha, you'd be a wonderful coach. You should really pursue coaching." That simple sentence sparked something deep inside me. Suddenly, all the scattered parts of my identity came together. I remembered the words of Ralph Waldo Emerson: "Be yourself; everyone else is already taken."

And so, I stepped into the world of coaching. It wasn't just about learning a new skill—it was about being fully present with another human being in a sacred space of acceptance and non-judgment. Coaching isn't about giving advice; it's about walking alongside someone. It's a deeply human connection that transforms conversation into a tool for inner discovery. In this space, people feel safe enough to share their fears, dreams, and doubts without the fear of being judged. It is here that the heart opens, trust grows, and the age-old human longing to be truly understood—not merely heard—is gently met. The coach, through their pure presence, not just being a listener, like a mirror, reflects the facts that the client may not yet see.

Through purposeful questions, the coach awakens thought and stirs the soul—not to deliver quick answers, but to open vast new vistas of meaning and insight. The coach, by refraining from offering solutions, helps the individual to find the answers they seek outside, within themselves.

In this pure presence, silence plays a basic role; A mindful silence that invites intuition, clarity, and depth.

In this path, responsibility also takes on a new meaning; the client finds out that they are not victims of circumstance but creators of our future experiences.

In this relationship, vulnerability is not a sign of weakness, but it is a bridge to inner strength and personal growth.

Coaching is far more than a conversation. It is a human relationship that offers an opportunity for inner discovery: a return to one's authentic self. It challenges limiting beliefs and opens up fresh outlooks. With each step, it brings a person closer to their most genuine, most aware, and most peaceful self.

Through this journey, writing found its way back into my life—reigniting a cherished dream from my youth: to use the magic of words to create even a small ripple of change in the world; the dream of writing a book that doesn't just tell my story but becomes a companion for those who are thirsty for change, or those who are tired and worn out, who, while going through a difficult phase in the midst of the twists and turns of life, ask themselves: "Why and how did I get here? How can I survive this predicament?"

Thriving through Challenges

Now, just as I prepare to launch my long-held dreams through coaching, life hands me another test. On this sorrowful evening of June 15, 2025, I write these words from this somewhat calmer half of the world while my son faces war and fear in our homeland, Iran. War isn't just a word for me. It is an old wound from childhood, from eight years of air raid sirens and explosions that still echo in my bones. I braved immigration for freedom and safety for my children—yet now, what I fled seems to have found them.

But this time, I've decided not to hide from fear. I will see it, accept it, embrace it—and turn it into strength. If I must carry a scar, let it also carry the mark of growth. Pausing for a moment, and through a fleeting glance at half a century of my life—at moments of uncertainty, illness, immigration, anxiety, and loneliness—I remind myself that life has never been and will be predictable. It has its own rhythm, and we must find our way to flow with it, so that the hardship weighs less on us.

I believe that my son, my friends, my people, and my country will emerge stronger, wiser, and more noble from this trial. They will discover new meaning in these painful days. As Haruki Murakami wrote in *Kafka on the Shore*:

"When you come out of the storm you won't be the same person who walked in. That's what this storm's all about."[1]

Coaching and writing became the two wings that lifted me. In entering these realms, I've learned that life is not easy. It can be sometimes brutal, dark, signless, and even overwhelming. But I believe in the human spirit—vast and limitless: If we open our eyes and truly desire it, paths will appear.

I learned that every crisis is rocky ground—but fertile soil for seeds of transformation. That peace doesn't come from escaping or avoiding pain, but by facing it, accepting it, and searching for meaning within it.

I discovered that old beliefs can be revisited, rethought, and a new path can be created before me.

I found out that in an uncertain world, what sustains us is our inner stability: that quiet, kind voice in the soul that whispers:

"This journey, no matter how difficult, remains precious, for every moment offers a chance to touch meaning and begin anew."

---

1. Murakami H. (2005). *Kafka on the shore*. Vintage International. (Original work published 2002)

Whispers of the Soul

About the Author

Gooya (Raha) Ghiasi, born in July 1975 in the alleys of Shiraz, surrounded by the fragrance of orange blossoms and the sound of Hafez's poetry. From birth, she was called "Raha"—a name that means freedom in Persian—and freedom became a part of her identity. She found her soul's meanings with traditional music strings and books. Despite many obstacles, she entered the world of cosmetology in her twenties. Since her love for learning was an inseparable part of her being, interacting with people and hearing their life stories added a fresh depth to her perspective. After raising her children and later through immigration, she launched online book circles that guided her toward the transformative path of coaching: a journey from within, toward meaning. Today, Raha is dedicated to using coaching as a tool for deep personal growth. She believes that every individual has the capacity to shine and create a life that aligns with their authentic values. Still, many people forget their inner power amidst the twists and turns of challenges and limiting beliefs.

She considers coaching as a way to revive this power and create sustainable change in life. Others describe her as a person with influential speech, patient, strong, kind, and responsible. She loves nature, color, art, poetry, books, music, and the silent beauties of life. Her vision is a world where every human rediscovers the timeless truth within their soul and experiences a conscious, balanced, and meaningful life. She believes that every inner shift creates a ripple of outer transformation—a model for today and a light for tomorrow.

Ways to Contact with the Author:

✉ rahaghiasi.coach@gmail.com
📷 Rahaghiasi.coach

A Woman's Transformation from Teacher to Coach

Azam Iraji

A Woman's Transformation from Teacher to Coach

Azam Iraji

Professional Business Coach, Founder of Life & Gold Academy in Iran and Turkey

My Voice Remained in the Hallways...

My voice still lingers in the school's hallways, caught between the wooden classroom boards and the scattered particles of chalk in the winter air. Sometimes, in moments of reflection, I can hear myself calling out a student's name or explaining a concept with passion—infused with the fervor of a teacher who believes that education is liberation.

I am a woman—not just on my birth certificate, but in the very fabric of my being. I was only eighteen when I became a wife, and at that same age, I became a mother. While juggling my studies, teaching, and life, I realized that my life wasn't going to wait for me. Simultaneously, I became a mother, a wife, and a teacher, stepping onto the challenging path of creating "myself." During those years, while most of my peers were still dreaming of a vague future, I was already standing my ground—amidst the classroom blackboard, the exam papers of my students, the baby bottle, the office, and half-finished dreams.

More than three decades have passed since those days—

three decades of experience as a mother, wife, educator, speaker, mentor, entrepreneur, and seeker on an endless quest for meaning. Looking back now, I see that I was immersed in all my roles; each one was simply a different garment worn by me. I was a woman who was shattered and rebuilt repeatedly. There was no one there to ask, "Are you ready?" My understanding and knowledge, my family structure, the social environment around me, and perhaps my destiny—my mission and my path of growth—shaped my life this way. Life kept moving forward, and I had to keep pace, creating my roles as I went. In those years, no one asked, "What do you want to be?" But in the silence, I chose to stay and build. I was a full-time student, a full-time teacher, a full-time mother, a full-time wife, and a supportive daughter to my family. I never understood where I found all that strength; I just knew I had to keep moving forward.

For years, I believed my mission was teaching. I loved the classroom and that golden moment when a student's eyes light up with understanding—a deep comprehension that no grade can measure. I experienced not only teaching and lecturing but also held various key managerial and executive positions, from mathematics to computer science, in technical schools, universities, vocational centers, and lecture halls for men and women seeking entrepreneurship, personal development, and business skills. I taught for years, learned how to build, and taught others to do the same.

Yet a voice always echoed in the depths of my mind: "Azam,

where are you in all of this?" It felt as if, amidst all these roles, my own self had been left behind—somewhere between the blackboards, the formulas, and the evaluation forms; a layer of me had fallen silent. This is the starting point of my story: the story of a woman who entered a multi-role world at eighteen, only to realize years later that truly living begins by returning to the silenced voice within.

Where the Path Changed

About ten years ago, at the peak of my career in the gold and jewelry industry—a business I had started alongside my teaching—I felt I could no longer continue in the same way. From the outside, my life appeared to be a model of success: a high income, a luxurious home, and a strong social standing. But inside, a tired, sometimes sad and silent woman was screaming. At that exact moment when I wanted to stop, it was as if life's genie worked its magic in its own way. That synchronicity still feels like a dark and mysterious labyrinth to me.

The decision to immigrate was sudden, made without any prior planning or preparation, like an unexpected death. Yet for me, it became a turning point—a golden moment behind a veil of pain and hardship; the day I had to fit my entire life into a forty-kilogram suitcase. I later realized that immigration is like a conscious death. That moment shook me to my core. I asked myself, "If I were to leave this world right now, what would remain of me?" I left everything behind: my house, my luxurious life, my cook, my housekeeper, my driver, my status, my language, my friends, my family, and even a part of my former identity. In exchange, it felt as though I gained something far more valuable: myself.

For me, immigration wasn't merely a change of geography; it was a profound experience that, like death, stripped everything from me only to return me to my true self. Imagine, after thirty years of living in comfort, stability, and a privileged social position, your only asset suddenly becomes a forty-kilogram suitcase. Behind you lies a lavish home, a successful business, an extended family, and an established image of yourself. Ahead of you lies an unknown country, an unfamiliar language, foreign laws, and an overwhelming sense of alienation. During those days, amidst the COVID-19 pandemic and closed borders, I said goodbye not only to my homeland but also to a version of "Azam." The woman who had sacrificed herself to social structures through various roles for years began to rediscover herself in the heart of that apparent catastrophe.

When the Suitcases Became Heavier Than a Lifetime...

That day, I had only one suitcase—not out of poverty, but out of detachment. I was always involved in charitable work for years and had always defined life's meaning as "to serve" and now I was suddenly faced with the starkness of a profound question: "Have I truly lived?"

It was the time of COVID; borders were closed, the world

was breathless, and my heart was restless. There I was, my children, an old suitcase, a plane with an uncertain departure, and a new life for which I had no plans. That was where the first spark ignited—not just the spark of immigration, but the flame of returning to myself. The seed of coaching was planted in my mind during those same years. I didn't yet know what it was called, but I understood that I had to see anew, understand anew, and be anew.

Coaching: Not a Profession, but a Return to Self

My first encounter with coaching felt like discovering a new world. When I took my first course, I was shocked. It was as if I had been viewing my life through filters I had constructed for years. I was so profoundly shaken that I began training at five different academies simultaneously, each with a unique approach. But coaching wasn't just about training; every coaching session became a journey within. In each professional conversation, I grew closer to a new layer of myself. Breathing in the coaching room was unlike any of my previous experiences. In that space, I wasn't a teacher, a mother, or a manager; I was simply myself. And how strange that true self felt.

This discovery was so profound, so striking, and so awakening that I could no longer go back. I became ravenous for learning, like someone who had just tasted freedom. I learned the techniques, but more importantly, with every exercise, every session, and every conversation, I rediscovered a piece of myself. For me, coaching wasn't just a skill; it was a mirror, a lantern, a compass. My sessions weren't only for my clients; each time, I journeyed inward alongside them. Many times, in the midst of a client's story, my own tears have fallen—not from weakness, but from encountering a silent truth within myself.

This path became so serious and life-saving that, within four years, I conducted over ten thousand hours of individual and group coaching sessions with clients from around the world. Simultaneously, I expanded my journey of self-discovery. I completed courses on the Enneagram[1] of Personality in reputable international academies and recognized aspects of my past in every personality type. In courses on Depth Psychology, I uncovered layers of my unconscious. This exploration led me to Astrology—not for prediction, but for reflection on our unique roles in the cosmos, to understand the secret order of the universe, and my place within it. Grasping archetypes, cycles, the mystery of time, and the cosmic influences on the human psyche provided me with the depth to comprehend, accept, and find a common language between universe and myself.

This perspective became a bridge connecting Eastern wisdom, modern psychology, and coaching. I learned that when a person sees themselves clearly, they also perceive the world more accurately. All of this served one purpose: to get to

---

1. A personality typing system that categorizes individuals into nine types, each with distinct motivations, fears, and behavioral patterns. The Enneagram serves as a tool for self-discovery and for gaining a deeper understanding of others.

know Azam—not the version others saw, but the woman lost between roles, responsibilities, and apparent successes. Today, when my clients sit across from me, I am not just a coach; I am a mirror that has shattered and reassembled itself time and again. Coaching was my path back to myself, to meaning, and to the light.

At eighteen, Azam became a mother, studied, and taught. At thirty, she was both an entrepreneur and a beloved teacher. At forty, she immigrated, started from scratch, and confronted her true self. During one coaching session, a single sentence came to mind that changed her path: "You fought for years to build a life, but you forgot to live it."

The Birth of a Holding Company from the Heart of a Crisis

For me, immigration was not just a geographical relocation; it shattered a familiar order, detached me from my comfort zone, and confronted a self that had been hidden for years under layers of "shoulds" and "roles." In the early days, Turkey was neither heaven nor hell; it was simply a silent land. No one knew me, my past, or my successes. But right there, within the walls of a simple rented house and at a small desk, far from the amenities and luxuries of my past, a decision was made: to create again. This time, it was not out of necessity, but with awareness; not for survival, but for meaning.

I conceived the Life & Gold Holding Company in my mind while everything was still uncertain. It was a bold combination of what I knew and what I believed in: the world of gold and jewelry, where I had years of experience, and the world of coaching, in which I had immersed myself deeply.

The first steps were slow. I faced an unfamiliar language, an unfamiliar market, and sometimes even unfamiliar tastes. But I had faith—not in immediate success, but in the rightness of the path. Every conversation, every partnership, every client, and every student contributed to building this holding company piece by piece. Today, as I sit at my meeting table and lead coaching classes at the Life & Gold Academy in Iran and Turkey, I realize that I didn't just build a business; I rebuilt myself.

I am a woman who has fallen, failed, and risen again, always moving forward. I have witnessed the true meaning of growth not on a profit and loss chart, but in the tears of a client, the smile of a student, and the courage of a colleague to make a fresh start. Today, after six years of immigration and starting over, managing the Life & Gold Holding Company and the Life & Gold Coaching Academy is the embodiment of a new life—one forged from a fusion of who I was, who I am, and who I am called to be. On this path, I am not alone; my children, colleagues, students, and clients are all part of this shared human journey, each living their own story of personal and professional growth.

I am no longer just a teacher or a coach; I am a woman who has lived this path: a journey from immigration to rebuilding, from raising a child to building a team, and from confronting the darkness within me to transforming it into light. The Life & Gold Holding Company and the Life & Gold Academy are not merely businesses; they embody the narrative of my life—a story of conscious courage, of creating something from nothing and finding rebirth in the heart of crisis.

Spirituality and Coaching: Two Languages of One Truth

Throughout these years, my experience in coaching has connected me to deeper concepts of existence. In my darkest moments, coaching extended its hand to me. Yet, in the silence of my soul, when I could not even hear my own voice, spirituality rescued me. I do not mean to suggest that everyone who becomes a coach will find salvation, for true salvation occurs only when one desires it and consciously steps onto that path. For me, coaching became a bridge between mind and heart, between decision and intuition, between what I "should" do and what my "soul" is called to do.

No one asks when a strong woman gets tired or when a woman who is always busy last cried. I didn't ask either—not of myself or others—until the day came when I could no longer continue in the old way. On that day, no particular crisis had occurred; nothing external had happened. It was just an ordinary morning in a familiar foreign land, in a rented house, amidst the daily routines of immigration. But inside me, there was turmoil. Questions arose that I could no longer ignore:

- What is all this effort for?

- Who am I?
- If everything is taken from me, do I still remain "me"?

Coaching began with these questions, and slowly, spirituality found its way into our conversations. In every coaching session, I faced a layer of myself alongside my clients—sometimes a wounded self-esteem, sometimes suppressed anger, sometimes a little girl who still longed to be seen. But spirituality wasn't just present in the coaching room; it sometimes arrived in the silence after a session or in confronting the oldest wounds. It was there that I understood true courage doesn't always shout; sometimes it shines in the silence of surrender—quiet yet bright.

Conscious courage is the point where you accept that you don't know but continue anyway; you accept that you are in pain but don't give up; you accept that the future is uncertain but take one more step. For years, I was a person of prayer and active in charities and public benefit work, but coaching fundamentally changed my understanding and brought my spirituality down to earth. I found spirituality in listening without judgment, in respecting the silent space between two sentences, and in a question that arose from the heart needing no answer.

With coaching, I reconnected with my Creator—not through a new belief but by returning to myself: my authentic, honest, fearful, and luminous self. I realized then that coaching is not just a technique; coaching is an earthly prayer.

A Golden Life: From Pain to Meaning

From that eighteen-year-old woman to this fifty-year-old woman, I have come a long way. Today, I am the founder of two organizations dedicated to women's empowerment, entrepreneurship, business coaching, and personal development. I am still learning every day. The wounds sometimes reopen, and I still shed tears, but I am no longer afraid of failure. I have learned that nothing is as healing as "being yourself," and no summit holds meaning without passing through the valleys.

In closing, to the woman reading this chapter, I say: if you have drifted away from yourself along your path, do not be afraid. Immigrate—internally or externally. All it takes is the decision to pack your suitcase and take only what you truly need: honesty, courage, and a dream worth building.

If you are a woman juggling multiple roles, constantly moving between work, home, and your dreams, and if your voice sometimes gets lost in the noise of life, you are not alone. I have been there too—tearful in a foreign land, with a heart fluctuating between fear and hope, and a soul searching for meaning.

Today, with my entire being, I say: "You have the right to start over. You have the right to hear your own voice. You have the right to build a completely new life."

For me, being a coach means accompanying people who seek clarity amidst chaos. It means creating a space for authentic conversation, free from judgment and fear. It means teaching you to know your roots while remembering your wings. I am a woman who has failed many times, but each time I rose and became the creator of a new story—for myself and for the world around me.

A Woman's Transformation from Teacher to Coach

About the Author

Azam Iraji is a professional business coach, a personal and business transformation instructor, and the founder of the Life & Gold Holding Company and the Life & Gold Academy in Iran and Turkey. With over three decades of experience in education and personal development—spanning schools, universities, and lecture halls—she has consistently been an inspirational and influential voice on the path to empowerment. After years in teaching and educational and administrative management, Azam ventured into the gold and jewelry trade. As a female entrepreneur, she successfully ran a family business in Iran. A pivotal moment in her life came with a sudden immigration that brought both release and reinvention, during which she discovered coaching not merely as a profession but as a means of reconnecting with herself.

To date, Azam Iraji has conducted nearly ten thousand hours of individual and group coaching sessions. By integrating knowledge from various fields, including coaching, the Enneagram, positive psychology, and astrology, she has developed a unique approach to human growth. Currently, she serves as the director of the international Life & Gold Holding Company in Turkey and is the founder of the Life & Gold Academy in Iran and Turkey—a center dedicated to training, coaching, life and business skills development, human growth, and fostering conscious living. Azam is committed to her mission of empowering women in business and personal development, believing that women are the powerful and unique collaborators of the Creator of the universe.

Women make up half the world, and the other half is born from them and grows in their embrace.

Contact the author:

 Azam_iraji
 Azam_iraji
 Azam_iraji
 Azam_iraji
 +905526144748

Coaching as The Unseen Force Behind High-Performing Leaders

Mohsen Khaki

Coaching as The Unseen Force Behind High-Performing Leaders

Mohsen Khaki

Professional Coach and Branding Expert

Coaching: The Key to Regaining Power

Picture this: The CEO of a billion-dollar tech company sits in their office, gazing out over the city skyline. They've built an empire, yet something feels off. Despite their monumental achievements, they are battling decision fatigue, struggling to inspire innovation, and feeling increasingly disconnected from their executive team. The weight of their responsibilities seems unbearable. Their once-crystal-clear vision is clouded, and each day feels like a battle to keep the organization moving forward.

I remember one such CEO, a brilliant leader with a track record of success, yet visibly worn. He sat across from me, a silent struggle in his eyes. "I feel like I'm running on empty," he confessed, rubbing his temples. The tension in his voice was palpable. He wasn't just fatigued; he was fighting an internal war. The high-level meetings he once dominated now felt like tiresome routines, and despite his best efforts, his team seemed to be losing momentum. As his challenges mounted, he began considering drastic alternatives: hiring a new team, seeking traditional management consulting, anything to spark the change he so desperately needed. Yet nothing worked. His frustration deepened, and he found himself at a crossroads.

Now, imagine a different scenario: This same leader, after engaging with a professional coach, begins to navigate his organization with renewed clarity and confidence. His executive meetings, once mundane, evolve into high-impact discussions that ignite creativity and drive results. His vision sharpens, empowering him to take bold, calculated risks that strengthen his company's position in an increasingly competitive landscape.

This transformation isn't hypothetical—it's happening in real time across organizations worldwide. Elon Musk has also confirmed that he benefits from professional coaching and continuous team feedback at Tesla and SpaceX- a purposeful process that helps him maintain focus, manage decision fatigue, and pursue innovative technological strategies.[1]

In retrospect, I recall working with another CEO who was similarly drained by the constant grind of high-stakes decisions. He felt stuck in an endless cycle of burnout. In one of our early sessions, his face was etched with exhaustion. "I feel overwhelmed," he admitted, his voice laced with frustration. Over the course of six months, we implemented a structured coaching plan that focused on energy management, decision-making frameworks, and enhancing leadership presence. By the end of our work together, he had a renewed sense of purpose. His meetings became dynamic and productive, and

---

1. Wolner, M. (2023, April 13). *Coaching Elon Musk: Our first meeting was in space.* Medium.

his leadership transformed. I'll never forget when he looked me in the eye and said, "I finally feel like the leader my company needs." What was once a voice filled with doubt and indecision had gained conviction and clarity.

This is not a rare occurrence — it's a repeatable, scalable process that organizations worldwide are leveraging to cultivate high-performance leadership. Coaching has evolved from a personal development tool into a cutting-edge approach that drives organizational excellence, strategic agility, and continuous innovation.

The Critical Leadership Challenges of Today's Most Successful Organizations

Before diving deeper into how coaching functions as a transformative technology, let's explore the core challenges that even the most successful leaders face today. These issues have deep-rooted implications that require sustained intervention and strategic solutions. If left unaddressed, high-performing organizations risk stagnation or even decline.

1. **Decision Overload**: As leaders rise through the ranks, the complexity of their decisions increases exponentially. With millions – or even billions — of dollars at stake, the mental burden can lead to cognitive overload and analysis paralysis. McKinsey's study on decision-making highlights that leaders spend over 70% of their time making decisions, often weighing countless interdependent factors. The pressure of

balancing stakeholder expectations, market shifts, and business dynamics can be overwhelming, leading to mental fatigue.[1] If left unchecked, this can lead to poor decision-making that negatively impacts the bottom line.

2. **Scaling Leadership**: Organizational growth often outpaces the development of leadership capabilities. As companies expand, leadership frameworks lag, creating a vacuum that impedes growth. According to a Harvard Business Review survey, 62% of executives report struggling to develop leaders quickly enough to keep pace with their organizations' growth.[2] "Before you are a leader, success is all about growing yourself. When you become a leader, success is all about growing others."[3] Without effective leadership scalability, organizations hit a growth ceiling, stifling their overall performance.

3. **Innovation Stagnation**: Companies that once thrived on innovation can plateau if leaders fail to embrace new ways of thinking. Cognitive biases, such as status quo bias, block fresh views, preventing leaders from recognizing disruptive innovations.

---

1. McKinsey & Company. (2021). *Decision-making in the digital age.* McKinsey & Company.
2. Harvard Business Review. (2022). The *leadership development gap.* Harvard Business Review.
3. Jack Welch, former CEO of General Electric, renowned for his leadership and management strategies. This sentence appears in the book "*Winning,*" authored by Jack Welch and Suzy Welch in 2005.

Disruptive innovation refers to new ideas, products, or technologies that significantly alter or replace existing business models—often by offering simpler, more affordable, or more accessible alternatives. Research from Boston Consulting Group reveals that 55% of executives fail to embrace disruptive innovations due to entrenched perspectives on traditional business models.[1] Without innovation, companies risk becoming irrelevant in a rapidly evolving market.

4. **Organizational Misalignment**: One of the most critical challenges in leadership is the gap between an executive team's vision and the operational reality within the organization. Many executives assume their teams fully understand their strategic direction, but research shows nearly 50% of employees feel disconnected from their company's goals.[2] This misalignment fractures organizational cultures and undermines team performance.

5. **Emotional Resilience and Burnout**: Even the most capable leaders can succumb to burnout. The constant demands of leadership often lead to exhaustion, disengagement, and diminished effectiveness. Gallup's study reveals that 70% of leaders are at risk

---

1. Harnoss, J., & Baeza, R. (2019). *Overcoming the four big barriers to innovation success*. Boston Consulting Group.
2. Joly, H. (2023). How to Connect Employees to Your Company's Purpose. *Harvard Business Review*.

of burnout due to stress, lack of emotional support, and overwhelming workloads.[1] This impacts not only decision-making and interpersonal relationships but ultimately the performance of their organizations.

Challenge: What Keeps You Up at Night?

Before proceeding, take a moment to reflect on the leadership challenges you face:

- What is the biggest leadership challenge consuming your mental energy?
- If you could improve just one aspect of your leadership effectiveness, what would it be?
- How much is ineffective leadership costing your organization in terms of lost potential, opportunities, or performance?

Write down your answers. These reflections will guide us as we explore how coaching offers practical, scalable solutions to these common leadership dilemmas.

From Ancient Art to a Science-Backed Technology

Historically, coaching has been viewed as an intuitive, relationship-driven process focused on personal development. However, recent advancements in neuroscience and psychology have transformed it into a structured, evidence-

---

1. Wallop, H. (2025, June 3). Don't be so hard on your boss: They've just been promoted too far. *The Times*.

based methodology.[1] Today, coaching is not just an art but a science that enhances cognitive flexibility, emotional intelligence, and leadership effectiveness through measurable outcomes.

Neuroscientific research highlights how coaching activates key areas of the brain associated with decision-making and emotional regulation. Functional Magnetic Resonance Imaging (fMRI) studies reveal increased activity in the prefrontal cortex —the region responsible for strategic thinking, problem-solving, and impulse control —when individuals engage in coaching conversations.[2]

Psychological research further supports these findings. Carol Dweck's work on mindset theory demonstrates how coaching fosters a shift from a fixed mindset to a growth-oriented perspective, enabling leaders to embrace challenges, learn from failures, and continuously improve.[3]

Beyond individual transformation, coaching has been shown to drive measurable organizational success. A MetrixGlobal study found that executive coaching yielded a 788% return on investment (ROI), considering factors like increased

---

1. "The integration of neuroscience into coaching provides a deeper understanding of human behavior and enhances the effectiveness of coaching interventions." Dr. David Rock, Director of the NeuroLeadership Institute, in his article "SCARF: A Brain-Based Model for Collaborating with and Influencing Others".
2. Rock, D., & Page, L. J. (2022). *Coaching with the brain in mind: Foundations for practice*. Wiley.
3. Dweck, C. S. (2006). *Mindset: The new psychology of success*. Random House.

productivity and employee retention.[1]

Moreover, research indicates that businesses integrating coaching into leadership development programs are more successful in achieving strategic goals than those without a coaching culture.[2]

By merging insights from neuroscience, psychology, and business research, coaching has evolved into a scalable technology for leadership transformation. It is no longer a luxury but a necessity for high-performance organizations navigating complex, ever-changing environments.[3]

Case Study: The Chief Technology Officer (CTO) Who Transformed a Culture through Coaching

I once worked with a company's CTO. Despite his technical brilliance and expertise, he struggled to lead effectively. His teams lacked direction, and meetings often ended in confusion. Even with technological successes, the leadership structure did not foster collaboration or efficient decision-making.

In one pivotal session, he confided, "I know how to build great products, but I don't know how to build great teams." This admission marked a turning point. We implemented a

---

1. American University. (2025). *The ROI of executive coaching* [Report]. American University, Washington, DC.
2. World Finance. (n.d.). Leadership development through coaching: A case study. Retrieved June 8, 2025, from https://www.worldfinance.com/strategy/leadership-development-through-coaching-a-case-study
3. «Adaptability is about the powerful difference between adapting to cope and adapting to win." Max McKeown, author and business strategist, in his book *"Adaptability: The Art of Winning in an Age of Uncertainty"*.

structured leadership framework focused on active listening, decision-making models, and high-impact questioning techniques. Within six months, the results were remarkable:

- Employee engagement increased by 32%, fostering a more collaborative environment.
- Project efficiency improved by 27%, resulting in significant savings in operational costs.
- A succession plan was developed to ensure leadership continuity.

One day, he walked into our session with newfound energy. "For the first time, my team isn't just following orders, they're bringing ideas to the table," he said. This shift in leadership was profound. Coaching unlocked not only his potential but also that of his team.

A Framework for Sustainable Leadership Transformation

Leadership development, especially at the executive level, cannot be a one-time event but a continuous process of reflection, learning, and adaptation. As organizations encounter increasing volatility, their leaders must evolve to navigate these challenges effectively.

Consider the case of a Senior Vice President (VP) of Sales I worked with who struggled with his leadership effectiveness. He aimed to confidently lead his team and drive better performance outcomes. Through our sessions, we identified that his over-reliance on micromanaging was hindering his team's autonomy and development.[1]

Together, we explored various options for empowering his team and ultimately decided on a more hands-off, results-oriented approach. He committed to delegating key responsibilities and investing in his team's professional development. Within six months, his team's sales performance increased by 25%, and employee turnover dropped by 15%.

The transformation was about improving performance and creating a sustainable leadership framework capable of driving long-term success.

Coaching as the Catalyst for Continuous Leadership Evolution

Leadership isn't static; like technology, it must evolve to keep pace with changes in the business environment. To keep your leadership "software" up to date, regular reflection, feedback, and refinement are essential.

Exercise: Debugging Your Leadership Code

Just as software requires regular updates, so does leadership. Reflect on the following questions:

- Where are the "bugs" in your leadership style that prevent you from performing at your best?

---

1. "The function of leadership is to produce more leaders, not more followers." Ralph Nader, American political activist, in his book *"The Seventeen Traditions."*

- What outdated mental models limit your effectiveness as a leader?
- If you could implement a leadership upgrade, what would it look like?

Choose one area to "update" this week. Write down a concrete action, then take immediate steps to implement it. Track your progress over time.

The Next Frontier: Coaching for the Future

The next five years will present even more challenges and opportunities for leaders in high-performing organizations. Here are some key trends that will shape the future of leadership:

1. **Hyper-Agility**: The ability to pivot quickly in response to market shifts will be critical. Leaders must remain nimble and adaptable while maintaining focus on their long-term objectives.[1]

2. **Human-Centered Leadership**: Leadership is shifting from being purely KPI-driven—that is, focused on Key Performance Indicators like sales targets, productivity rates, or revenue growth— to prioritizing employee engagement, well-being, and a shared sense of purpose. In this new landscape, emotional intelligence will emerge as a

---

1. "It is not the strongest of the species that survive, nor the most intelligent, but the one most responsive to change." Charles Darwin, English naturalist, in his book "*On the Origin of Species*"

key differentiator among high-performing leaders, enabling them to foster trust, motivation, and deeper connections within their teams.[1]

3. **Artificial Intelligence (AI) and Coaching Integration**: Soon, leaders will increasingly rely on AI-powered coaching platforms to enhance their decision-making. These platforms will offer real-time feedback, personalized coaching recommendations, and adaptive learning paths.

4. **Continuous Learning**: Organizations that invest in leadership development will outperform their peers. Companies prioritizing the growth of their leaders will be more resilient and better positioned to thrive in the face of disruption.

Challenge: The 5-Year Vision Alignment

Take a moment to reflect on your organization's future leadership. Where do you envision yourself and your team in five years?

- What will exceptional leadership look like in your organization?
- What changes must occur today to make that vision a reality?
- How will you ensure that leadership evolution continues

---

[1]. "Emotional intelligence is the sine qua non of leadership." Daniel Goleman, American psychologist, in his article "What Makes a Leader?" published in Harvard Business Review, 1998.

beyond this moment?

The New Imperative for Leadership Success

True leadership isn't just about keeping up; it's about staying ahead. Organizations that embed coaching into their culture not only develop better leaders but also build resilient, future-ready teams that thrive in an unpredictable world.

The future of leadership belongs to those who commit to continuous learning, adaptability, and intentional growth. Coaching serves as the catalyst that transforms challenges into opportunities, uncertainty into clarity, and leaders into game-changers.

Therefore, the real question isn't whether coaching is necessary; it's whether you're prepared to elevate your leadership, unlock your full potential, and shape the future.

Are you ready to take the leap?

Exercise: Unpacking Your Leadership Identity and Crafting Your Evolutionary Action Plan

1. Self-Reflection on Leadership Challenges

Take 15 minutes to reflect on your leadership journey.[1] Use the following prompts to guide your introspection:

- What leadership challenge consumes most of your

---

[1]. "Knowing others is intelligence; knowing yourself is true wisdom." Lao Tzu, ancient Chinese philosopher, in the book "*Tao Te Ching*", Chapter 33

mental energy today?

Write down this challenge in detail. What feelings does it evoke? Do you feel stuck, overwhelmed, or unclear about the next steps?

- When was the last time you felt truly energized in your leadership role?

Describe a specific moment when you were at your peak. What was different? What behaviors or actions did you exhibit that aligned with your best self?

- What assumptions or beliefs about leadership might be limiting your growth?

List any assumptions or mindsets that could be influencing your decisions. These may include biases or outdated mental models you've unknowingly held.

2. Critical Thinking Challenge: Disrupting Your Current Leadership Approach

Now that you've reflected on your current leadership state, it's time to challenge your thinking.

- What aspect of your leadership needs to be disrupted for you to move forward?

Identify one key area of your leadership approach that no longer serves you, such as decision-making, emotional resilience, or innovation.

- Imagine you are coaching yourself as a high-performance leader. What questions would you ask to unlock new perspectives?

Adopt a coaching mindset. For example, ask: "What would be possible if I stopped doing X? How might I approach this challenge from a different angle?"

3. Action Plan: Moving from Insight to Execution

The final step is crafting a concrete action plan that reflects the insights gained through this exercise.[1]

- Choose one insight from the previous sections that you believe will have the greatest impact on your leadership effectiveness.

What change can you make immediately to begin shifting your leadership approach? This could be a mindset shift, a new habit, or a behavior change.

- Define specific, measurable actions to implement this change in the next 30 days.

For example: "I will delegate at least two projects to my team members this month to empower them and focus on high-level strategy."

- How will you track your progress and hold yourself accountable?

Outline the steps you will take to monitor your progress. Will you check in with a colleague, reflect weekly, or keep a

---

1. "An idea not coupled with action will never get any bigger than the brain cell it occupied." Arnold Glasow, American humorist in *"The Wit and Wisdom of Arnold Glasow,"* 2004.

leadership journal?

4. Coaching for "Aha Moments" and Continuous Evolution

The key to sustainable leadership evolution is regular reflection. To ensure you continue evolving, commit to one of the following practices:

- **Create a feedback loop:** Set up regular sessions with a coach or mentor where you can unpack your leadership challenges and track your growth over time.
- **Embrace learning:** Identify a leadership development book, course, or seminar that you will engage with in the next six months to expand your leadership toolkit.

5. What Does Leadership Look Like For You in Five Years?

Use the insights from this chapter and your action plan to envision your future as a leader.[1] How will your approach to leadership evolve over time, and what lasting impact will this evolution have?

Thank you for engaging with this chapter of the book. If you would like to receive a free step-by-step guide on "Leadership Coaching," I encourage you to visit my website at ***www.mohsenkhakicoaching.com*** (Articles section).

---

1. "Leadership is the capacity to translate vision into reality." Warren Bennis, American scholar and leadership expert, *On Becoming a Leader*. 1989.

Additionally, if you're interested in enhancing your learning and having the opportunity to work directly with me as your coach, please send your request to ***mohsenkhakicoaching@yahoo.com*** or visit the "Services/Request Coaching Sessions" section on my website.

Coaching as The Unseen Force Behind High-Performing Leaders

About the Author

Mohsen Khaki is an author, an internationally certified professional coach by the International Coaching Federation (ICF), and a branding specialist. He began his professional journey at the age of eighteen by teaching English. Changes in his career path started in the early years when he decided to switch to teaching English after graduating from university with a degree in mechanical engineering. The initial failure in his entrepreneurial journey gave Mohsen a profound perspective on the challenges and opportunities for strengthening his brand. With over two decades of experience in language teaching and educational consulting, Mohsen built a strong reputation in preparing students for international exams, especially IELTS, through thousands of impactful workshops. His deep understanding of human learning, communication, and motivation naturally sparked a desire to create greater value beyond the classroom. This passion led him to explore the fields of business management, marketing and sales, branding, and psychology. Eventually, he pursued specialized international coaching programs, integrating his teaching expertise with coaching methodologies to support business development and personal transformation.

He is now active as a successful professional coach at the global level and, relying on the experience of conducting thousands of hours of specialized coaching and hundreds of international consultations, he assists business owners, leaders, and organization managers in creating a sustainable leadership framework, transformative action plan, agile strategy, growth mindset, and an innovative culture in business and increasing team productivity. In addition, he has designed and implemented numerous programs and workshops aimed at identifying and nurturing individual and professional talents. In this way, he helps people, including organization employees, to advance their personal and professional paths in the best possible way by identifying their strengths. Mohsen is passionate about learning, studying, his own personal growth and that of others, and has a keen interest in sports, travel, and music.

You can contact him through the following ways:

For coaching:

🌐 www.mohsenkhakicoaching.com
✉ mohsenkhakicoaching@yahoo.com
in mohsenkhakicoaching

For IELTS:

🌐 www.mohsenkhaki-ielts.com
✉ ieltskhaki@gmail.com
in IELTS Khaki

The Third Seat
Where Coaching Takes Flight

Mohammad Mehri

The Third Seat
Where Coaching Takes Flight

Mohammad Mehri
Flight Engineer, Mental Clarity Coach

Observing the Inner Flight

Clarifying the Objective Before the Journey Begins

Morning light softly streamed through the small window, slipping into the quiet cabin. The airplane stood still on the runway—silent, yet with a sleeping heart ready to awaken. I sat in the third seat—not at the controls, not making decisions. My role was to observe, to feel, and to read the signs.

The pilot and co-pilot were deep in preparation: checklists, system checks, conversations with the control tower. But something even more critical was unfolding—defining the destination into the flight management system.

Every flight without a clear destination and defined route is endless wandering. Before takeoff, the destination must be set, navigation coordinates precisely defined, and the route entered into the flight computer. Without this clarity, even the most skilled pilots would be flying aimlessly.

Coaching is no different. Each coaching session is like preparing for a flight. If we don't know exactly where the client wants to go, and if the mental journey map is unclear, the conversation turns into a drift through the skies of thought, ungrounded and directionless.

Like a flight plan, the goal of a coaching session must be clear, specific, and actionable.

At the beginning of every professional coaching session, the coach and client chart the course together:

- Where are we now?
- Where do we want to go?
- What points must we pass along the way?

Just as entering flight coordinates into an aircraft's navigation system is essential for the journey, coaching requires clearly defined mental coordinates—a shared understanding of the path ahead.

A Real Coaching Moment

One day, a young client sat across from me and said just one sentence: "I don't even know where to begin… I just feel like I'm falling behind."

If I had let the conversation continue in that vague, undefined space, it would've been like starting the plane's engines and lifting off—without knowing which direction to fly. So, gently, I helped him find clarity, like lighting up the runway before takeoff:

"What exactly would you like to focus on today?"

"If something were to shift by the end of our session, what

would make you feel more satisfied?"

"When you leave this room, what answer would you be glad to have found?"

Gradually, like checking vital parameters in a flight cockpit, the real objective emerged:

"I want to restructure my daily routine to feel like I'm making progress."

That became our flight's destination. And from that moment, the actual mental journey began.

Just as every flight checklist is meaningless without a set destination, every coaching question or thoughtful pause loses its power in the fog of uncertainty.

The third seat—the observer's seat—is where the journey begins. It's where we make sure the client has a clear mental destination, where we map out the path before soaring, and where we ensure we're aligned and heading in the right direction.

That's when real coaching takes off.

Before the Takeoff: The Need for Safety to Fly

Creating Safety and Trust in Coaching

The engines had started. That initial low vibration—resonating through the cabin like the heartbeat of the aircraft awakening for a long journey—filled the space. Everything was ready for movement, yet something even more essential than gauges and systems was still needed. Because once the engines are running, all flight controls must be checked—not just for function, but for trust: trust that they will guide the aircraft safely through the sky.

I sat in the third seat. No commands to give, no buttons to press—only to observe, to listen, to feel.

In aviation, the start of the engines does not mark the beginning of the flight. These early moments are critical. They're about establishing alignment, confidence, and trust: trust in the systems, in the flight controls, in the parameters, and in the aircraft itself—the very thing that will carry us toward our destination. Without that trust, no flight is truly safe, no matter how flawless everything may appear.

Coaching is much the same. A space of psychological safety must be created before diving into deep conversations or forming any action or decision. A space where the client feels seen, heard, and—most importantly—free from judgment. Only then can the mind become ready to take flight.

Safety isn't built through words alone. It's presence that creates safety—the true presence of the coach, marked by attentive stillness, patient silences, nonjudgmental glances, and questions that carry the scent of curiosity and kindness.

A Real Coaching Moment

One of my clients began the session in a very closed and guarded manner. Their body language conveyed a lack of complete trust: clasped hands, brief and fleeting glances, and vague sentences. At that moment, I remembered that my role wasn't to ask many questions but to create a space where they could open up.

I sat with full presence and started with a few short but sincere sentences: "I am here just to listen to you. Whatever you choose to share with me today is completely safe." No pressure, no rush, no judgment.

A few minutes later, their hands unclasped, their glances lengthened, their tone softened, and the session began more authentically than I had imagined.

In flight, no one allows takeoff without ensuring the health of the engines and systems. Similarly, in coaching, no professional coach engages in awareness-building or action before establishing safety.

The third seat means hearing the hidden tremors of the engines, seeing the doubt in the client's eyes, and respecting the time needed for trust to build. This is the beginning of the real journey in coaching.

When Silence Speaks Louder Than Words

Active Listening

The airplane, after a gentle takeoff, gradually ascended into the sky. A deep silence permeated the cabin; a silence full of sounds. In those moments, every sound had meaning: the engine's vibration, the gentle tension in the controls, the short conversations between the pilots and air traffic control. And I, in the third seat, was neither engrossed in commands nor busy with displays; I was listening with my whole being.

Listening in flight isn't just about hearing conversations; it's about perceiving hidden sounds: subtle, minute changes, faint body vibrations, or even silences that last too long. Every sound can signal something yet unseen.

Hearing beyond the client's words means understanding their silences, paying attention to pauses that hold unspoken thoughts, and sensing changes in their tone when they discuss something heavy for them. A coach isn't just a listener of words; a coach perceives the client's entire being. The actual presence of a coach in a session means listening with eyes, heart, feeling, and one's whole being.

A Real Coaching Moment

In one coaching session, my client began discussing their job. Their words were positive: "It's good," "I'm satisfied," "Everything's okay," but their tone was cold, their body still, and their voice monotonous. I would have been misled if I had focused solely on their words; however, authentic listening revealed a different story. Gently, I said, "There's something in your voice that suggests you're not enjoying your job. Would you like to talk a bit more about how you feel?"

That brief pause and simple question opened the door to a world hidden behind "everything's okay."

Failing to notice small vibrations in flight can signal the onset of a silent crisis. In coaching, overlooking subtle signs can mean missing a valuable opportunity for awareness.

The third seat represents the ability to hear what others do not, to be present not just with ears but with the heart, and to understand silences and words. Sometimes, the most powerful changes occur in the silence that someone has dared to listen to truly.

In the Heart of the Sky, I Found the Secret of the Earth

Evoking Awareness

The airplane had reached cruising altitude. The earth spread below us like a vast map; rivers gleamed like silver threads, roads vanished into the mountains, and cities appeared as small, silent specks from this height. In the third seat, with a calm gaze, I observed the world. What could not be seen from the ground was clearly visible here.

The higher we ascended, the more hidden patterns became apparent: the bends of rivers, the layout of roads, and points that seemed chaotic from the ground now took on new meaning from this altitude.

In coaching, the journey to the altitude of awareness carries the same significance.

When a client is overwhelmed by daily problems and intense emotions, the world can seem fragmented and meaningless.

However, the coach, through right questions and deep presence, helps them rise above their circumstances, allowing them to distance themselves from the immediacy of events and discern the underlying patterns.

Awareness involves discovering previously unseen connections; it means understanding that today's decisions are rooted in yesterday's beliefs; it means recognizing how seemingly unrelated behaviors have collectively formed a path that has led us to this point.

A Real Coaching Moment

In one session, my client repeatedly expressed feelings of job fatigue. While the initial issue appeared to be the high volume of work, deeper exploration revealed that the root of their fatigue was not simply too much work, but rather the fear of saying no and the need for others' approval. They made this connection themselves, and their face brightened as if they were seeing the hidden patterns of their life for the first time from a higher altitude. When flying, distancing yourself from the ground allows you to see the patterns of the forest instead of individual trees. In coaching, elevating a client's awareness enables them to recognize their mental patterns and derive new meaning from their life.

The third seat represents an invitation to a higher perspective—an opportunity to uncover what remains hidden on the surface of life and to discover secrets that only become apparent in the heart of the sky.

The Silence of the Mind in the Turbulence of the Sky

Presence in the Moment

The cockpit has many instruments: lights, screens, warning sounds, and subtle movements of the displays. As a flight engineer, I have learned to quiet my mind. Amid every light and sound, one thing must remain clear: focus.

During one flight, a continuous sound from an insignificant alarm kept repeating. It wasn't dangerous or critical—just distracting. I realized that if my mind reacted to it even for a moment, I would fail to analyze the main system. That was when I understood that mental control itself is a crucial flight skill.

Coaching is similar. As the client speaks, the coach's mind begins to race with thoughts: "What should I say now?", "Why did they get upset?", "What question should I ask next?", "The session time is running out..." These distractions are real, but the coach must become invisible—not to the client, but to their own thoughts.

A Real Coaching Moment

In one of my sessions, the client was speaking, but my mind was preoccupied with the sound of the window not being fully closed. I wanted to get up and close it, but I stayed put. I reclaimed my focus and presence. I just sat there. At that very moment, I heard a sentence from the client that changed the direction of the session: they quietly mumbled, "I wish I could tell them what's truly on my mind..."

Coaching is a profession of full presence; not just physical presence, but also mental, emotional, and sensory presence with one's whole being. Sometimes, the hardest thing in the world is precisely this: silencing a mind that wants to distract you.

The Art of Silent Observation

Objectivity and Presence in the Coaching Mindset

The aircraft was cruising above the clouds. The sun hovered near the horizon, casting a golden hue across the cockpit panels. The soft hum of the systems and the calm of the cabin invited a reflective stillness. In that stillness, something subtle—but significant—unfolded.

A brief exchange took place between the pilot and co-pilot. It was a simple matter of navigation, but their responses revealed two very different styles: one confident and assertive, the other cautious and analytical. Instinctively, I wanted to offer my opinion—to choose sides, to suggest who might be "right." But I paused. I remembered my role: not to intervene, not to judge, but simply to observe. If I spoke, my own perspective could disrupt the delicate operational rhythm between them. That moment taught me something essential: True presence means letting go of the need to interpret—and learning to witness with open eyes, open ears, and an open heart.

In coaching, the same principle applies. The coach is not a judge, a savior, or even a teacher. They are a neutral presence—a witness to the unique landscape of another person's mind. A good coach holds space for difference: in culture, in beliefs, in decisions, in thought patterns, and even in body language. Just because a certain path worked for us does not mean it is the right one for someone else. Each person's mind is a world of its own—never meant to be compared, judged, or defined by another.

A Real Coaching Moment

In one of my sessions, the client shared stories about their upbringing—disciplinary practices that felt harsh or even emotionally restrictive to me. However, I noticed something: for them, those very practices had created a sense of *safety*. If I had judged, even silently, I might have triggered shame or defensiveness. Instead, I listened. I didn't analyze or ask probing questions that involved critique. In that space, the client quietly said: "No one's ever really listened to me without trying to fix me."

In the cockpit, my job is to build understanding between two different minds—not to take sides or construct walls of judgment. In coaching, that responsibility becomes even clearer. The coach acts like a mirror polish in the third seat—they don't amplify or suppress anything; they simply reflect what is.

That's what objectivity looks like: a deep respect for the other person's experience and complete acceptance of their truth, without the need to reshape it.

Engineering Inner Transformation

Facilitating the Client's Growth

The airplane began its gentle descent from cruising altitude. The speed had slowed, and the body of the aircraft glided smoothly beneath the clouds. In quiet coordination, the pilot and co-pilot carried out their pre-landing checks. From the third seat, I watched these moments with quiet awe—moments that seemed simple on the surface, but held within them a mastery of skill, experience, and deep awareness. A successful landing is never an accident. It is the result of careful observation, sound decisions made at critical moments, and countless small and large adjustments throughout the journey. Landing is the transition from soaring through clouds to touching the earth once again—but with a deeper understanding, a clearer view, and wisdom shaped by the journey.

In coaching, the landing moment is when the client begins to integrate their insights and chart a path forward. It's the phase where the coach ensures the client doesn't leave the session with just a *"good feeling,"* but with a clear plan for real, sustainable change. This is where the coach's role comes full circle—not as the hero of the story, but as the one who prepares the launchpad for the client's growth.

A Real Coaching Moment

In one session, after a deep mental journey, the client concluded that they needed to pay more attention to their personal interests.

However, if the session had ended there, this insight would soon be lost in the daily hustle. So, through my questions, I helped them transform this awareness into action: "What's the first step you'll take today?" "What will help you stay on track?" "What's your plan if a challenge arises?"

With these questions, their awareness took root, created movement, and translated into reality.

In aviation, a successful landing results from proper journey management. In coaching, real change stems from effectively guiding the growth process.

The third seat represents observing the moment of landing—not as the end of a journey, but as the beginning of a new one. It embodies the belief that every touch of the ground is an opportunity for higher ascents, reflecting the quiet and profound engineering of inner transformation.

My work is merely to dust off a glass; a glass between an individual and themselves through which they can meet their second self: the one who they are (in the first seat) and the one who they can be (in the second seat). The individual in the third seat serves merely as an observer of this meeting, tasked with clarifying the inner mirror. This is their mission.

The Third Seat
Where Coaching Takes Flight

About the Author

Mohammad Mehri is a flight engineer and mental clarity coach. He began his career in aerospace engineering, a field where precision, observation, and unbiased analysis are vital. After years of experience in aviation, Mohammad had a profound realization: many of life's flights, before they fail in the sky, crash in people's minds. With this insight, Mohammad embarked on a new journey into the realm of personal growth and coaching.

Today, with the precision of a flight engineer, Mohammad Mehri assists individuals in re-evaluating their mental maps, identifying hidden obstacles, and designing clear, effective paths to success. He is the author of the book *Coaching*

Insights, available on Amazon. This book combines the science, art, and philosophy of coaching, narrating a journey from the harsh realities of life to the hopeful horizons of possibility.

Mohammad believes that coaching, much like flight engineering, is not merely about direct guidance; it is a science centered on fostering growth and facilitating self-leadership in others. Through his "Mental Clarity Coaching" method, he helps individuals discover their clear path amidst chaos and countless choices, empowering them to move forward with confidence.

For those who dare to embark on a new journey in their lives, Mohammad is not just a coach; he is a thought partner and an architect of inner transformation.

Connect with the Author:

- Mohamadmehri.coach
- Mohamadmehri.coach
- Mohamadmehri.coach@gmail.com
- (+98) 935 898 9891

In Search of the Meaning of Self

Dr. Maryam (Elnaz) Rahimzadeh

In Search of the Meaning of Self
Dr. Maryam (Elnaz) Rahimzadeh
Inner Transformation Coach, Self-Actualization Instructor, and Dentist

In Pursuit of Life's Meaning

I remember from my teenage years always asking myself, "Is there truly justice in the world? How can one claim justice exists when people's shares of happiness, opportunities, and comfort are so disparate and unequal?"

I yearned to view existence from a higher vantage point, beyond daily life. I wanted to understand why we live and whether the suffering endured by people worldwide truly holds a purpose.

In this quest, I was deeply captivated by a recurring theme across various mystical and cultural traditions, from East to West: a shared experience of oneness with existence, where love is recognized as the foundation of the world. This experience transcends the duality of pain and joy, embracing life as unified and sacred, and revealing the essence of humanity as rooted in joy and peace.

From Blossoming to Breaking

It was the last days of summer. After years away, I returned to the city of my childhood, this time as a dentistry student. I felt proud of myself and the diligence I had put into succeeding in the university entrance exam. I believed that the goal of my first two decades of life—learning how to live and build a bright future as an independent and capable individual—was finally being realized. However, this perception did not last long. Whenever I revisit those memories, I picture a fall: someone celebrating their ascent to a high peak, unaware that they will soon be thrown down from that very height.

Life in the dormitory was challenging and bore no resemblance to the comfort and security of home. My values and moral principles, which I meticulously guarded—such as refraining from gossip and ridiculing others—often left me feeling lonely in social gatherings. My study habits, accustomed to focusing on details, were ill-suited for the demanding university courses. Gradually, I sensed a change within me; it felt as if my zest for life was diminishing, and I lacked my former vitality and cheerfulness. I struggled to focus my mind, and my memory had severely declined. I didn't recognize this lifeless, incapable version of myself and felt lost, unsure of how to regain my former self. These confusing changes brought about a deep sense of shame that lingered for years, tormenting me. I felt as though I had lost my identity, as if my spirit had died. Unfortunately, it took a long time for me to realize I was suffering from depression. Just as my depression began to be treated, a tragic accident claimed the life of my brother, who was only 17. In the year or two before his passing, as he matured beyond childhood, our bond deepened more than ever. Whenever I returned home for the holidays, we had so much to talk about. Now, he was gone forever, and that haunting question echoed in my mind: "Why must we suffer so much? What is the purpose of all this pain and hardship that life sometimes imposes on us?"

A year later, I graduated and returned to Tehran, marking the beginning of a new chapter in my life: marriage and a career. After the great calamity and loss that had struck my family, I felt a strong need to take better care of my parents. Simultaneously, I was entering a new world that felt unfamiliar. Like many young people, I had spent the first 26 years of my life in education, and now I was stepping into the job market. I desperately needed a supporter and a secure anchor. I married a distant relative whose family I knew to some extent. It was during the early years of our marriage that I realized I had made the wrong choice and that our values were far apart. However, leaving the relationship felt like a daunting prospect. We both tried to improve our bond, navigating the ups and downs of our relationship.

The Fire of Passion

Entering the fourth decade of my life, with its successes and failures, a passion burned more intensely within me than ever before: to know and improve myself. This need and desire now found clearer answers. Classes and workshops, each approaching the deciphering of the human psyche from a different perspective, were more accessible, and many books on this subject were being translated and published. Jungian analytical psychology, which had gained significant popularity, provided excellent insights on how to explore myself, identify my thought and behavioral patterns, and restore balance. I experimented with various approaches, each addressing the complex structure of the human psyche from a different angle, to gain a deeper understanding of myself and those around me. From analytical psychology to transactional analysis, Acceptance and Commitment Therapy (ACT), free writing and journaling, meditation, various breathing techniques, dream analysis, and psychotherapy, my search for self-awareness continued. Each time, I discovered a piece of my puzzle and placed it in position.

The Spell of the Red Rose

It was the last days of autumn. COVID-19 was raging. Daily life had taken on a strange hue; we had grown accustomed to breathing through masks, sanitizing objects, and constantly monitoring statistics. In those turbulent days, I entered a new phase of my life that was filled with peace. I had separated and was living alone. Solitude and privacy had always been a sanctuary for me, and now I was experiencing and appreciating it more deeply and meaningfully than ever before.

The last day of autumn had always been a day of celebration for me, celebrating my birthday with friends and family, amidst the red pomegranates and watermelon of Yalda Night[1]. But that year, there was no gathering, no Hafez reading, and

---

1. Yalda Night: An ancient Persian festival celebrating the winter solstice, observed on the longest night of the year. Families gather to eat, read poetry (especially from Hafez), and tell stories, symbolizing the victory of light over darkness.

no joy of Yalda Night. Avoiding COVID and staying alive had become the top priority above everything else.

> It is not our calling to unravel the mystery of the red rose.
> Perhaps our calling is simply to be immersed in its enchantment.[1]

One Friday, a few days after my fortieth birthday, I woke up early, as usual, and began journaling. This practice helps me organize my thoughts and start my day with clarity. As I wrote, my attention was suddenly drawn to my hand. I felt the pen slipping between my fingers, and my hand was losing color. Suddenly, a terrible tremor seized my entire being. Overwhelming anxiety engulfed me. No matter how much I tried to warm myself, it was futile. It was a shocking experience that I had not anticipated, intensifying my anxiety. I had never felt this way before. "What a terrible state! Will I survive?"

Gradually, my perception of time and space shifted; each moment stretched into hours. My awareness fluctuated between illusion and reality until I completely detached from my surroundings. I saw my life from above, with relationships and concerns spread out below me like pieces of a small game.

"Life is a game; why have we forgotten this?" In that moment, it seemed an obvious truth that had been overlooked. We take life too seriously, so focused on realizing our ideal future that we forget to be present and enjoy what is; like actors in a play who have forgotten the stage and mistaken it for real life.

---

1. From a poem by Sohrab Sepehri, renowned Iranian poet and painter.

Slowly, the space around me transformed. I felt as if I had been cast alone into the middle of a galaxy, with no living creature nearby. Yet, this solitude deepened further. A voice within me said, "No, you haven't been thrown into space. There are no humans or living beings in the distant reaches either. You are at the beginning of creation."

It was just me and a lifeless world. At first, this solitude amused me: "How interesting! There's no one in the world but me." But soon, my feelings shifted: "No! It's not funny at all! How terrifying! And infinitely boring!"

I wished I could sleep to escape this nightmare, even for just a few minutes. I was willing to die, but I couldn't. I was "pure consciousness"—eternal and everlasting. In my despair, I reminded myself, "God cannot sleep or die." In those moments, my understanding of being God was simply pure solitude. How heavy and exhausting solitude is when there is no one else in the background. I began to realize how much the pleasure I had always derived from privacy and solitude depended on the presence of other human beings.

Gradually, my consciousness returned. I couldn't believe I was alive again, able to see the world as it once was and feel the vibrancy of life. I, who had loved solitude and privacy, had now, for the first time, tasted the shocking flavor of absolute solitude.[1]

---

1. This is a true story, briefly mentioned here. Readers interested in learning more details about the event are welcome to contact the author using the information provided at the end of the chapter.

Those difficult days passed slowly, and life gradually returned to normal, but one profound change occurred within me. My long search for the meaning of life and suffering had finally reached its end. A reality became clear to me—so clear that understanding the purpose of life no longer mattered. I still don't know the ultimate purpose of creation; I just know that I exist, and the knowledge that billions of other humans like me exist is enough. The nightmare of absolute solitude made me realize what a great blessing it is to be in the presence of others. Despite our many differences, we share commonalities: we all experience the ambiguity and uncertainty of life, we all know we have a limited opportunity to live, we all bear the burden of existence, and each of us experiences pain in some way. Our shared pains and sufferings create the deepest bonds.

Every human being is a unique entity with special abilities, talents, passions, and experiences, capable of solving others' problems, opening paths, or shining lights. Each person is a piece of a larger puzzle, and only when every piece is in place does the overall picture emerge. I had never been so interested in humanity. The wounds I had unknowingly sustained may have caused me to lose hope in people.

But now my interpretation had shifted; what I had been searching for was right here. The dark aspects of life that I had never been able to digest were gradually beginning to make sense. If there were no pain and suffering, no growth would arise. Within every challenge and every wound lies an opportunity—for the one who seeks solutions and for the one who offers help and support. Our role is to create meaning.

While we may have no control over the world and the events around us, one thing we can control is how we think, how we interpret events, the world around us, and ourselves, and how we act.

The more we become aware of ourselves—our thought patterns and behaviors—the more mastery and agency we gain. The constraints of life may always exist, but human choice can expand.

"Until you make the unconscious conscious, it will direct your life, and you will call it fate."[1]

I worked as a dentist for many years. Time and again, my patients expressed relief from pain or newfound confidence in their smiles after my treatments. While this always brought me joy, I felt something was missing. Many times, as a patient sat in the dental chair and I worked, a thought crossed my mind: "I wish I could do something for people's souls and minds, not just their bodies."

I often considered returning to university to study psychology, but this path didn't particularly appeal to me, and I would change my mind each time. However, a burning desire persisted. I wanted to help people trapped in the darkness of life change their outlooks. Years of self-exploration and navigating the complexities of the psyche had deepened my fascination

---

1. Carl Gustav Jung in his famous book, *Modern Man in Search of a Soul*, Translated by Fereydoon Faramarzi and Leila Faramarzi, published by Astan Quds Razavi Publications.

with this subject. I realized that we experience the world within ourselves; we can either change our circumstances and pursue our desires or choose our perspective when circumstances are beyond our control. Our mission in life is to build happiness and create meaning, guided by awareness and the delicate balance we establish between ourselves, others, and the universe.

"Everything can be taken from a man but one thing: the last of the human freedoms—to choose one's attitude in any given set of circumstances."[1]

Crossing the Threshold

For several years, the term "coach" became increasingly common; however, the fact that many individuals from diverse specialties identified as coaches made me skeptical. That changed when I discovered authentic coaching. The more I learned about coaching, the more fascinated I became; it is a modern process rooted in philosophy, psychology, management, communication sciences, and neuroscience. Its goal is to uncover their potential and nurture their creativity. Unlike teaching or consulting, which focus on knowledge transfer or providing solutions, coaching emphasizes strengthening self-awareness, responsibility, and creating internal solutions.

Each time I accompany a client in the process of exploring their thoughts, feelings, and behaviors, I embark on an adventurous

---

1. Viktor E. Frankl, in his masterpiece, *Man's Search for Meaning*, translated by Nehzat Salehian and Mahin Milani.

journey. At every step, I serve as a non-judgmental mirror, reflecting different dimensions of the person back to them so they can achieve greater integration with themselves.

A Glimpse into Coaching: Moments of Growth and Discovery

Sarah, one of my clients, was a brave and self-aware woman with whom I had worked for months. That morning, she was feeling very frustrated and angry with herself for her impulsiveness. During our session, we began to explore this issue. Sarah recalled that whenever she focused deeply on a task, she achieved success in a short period. This realization inspired her, and she decided to work more on her mindfulness.

As her face calmed, it suddenly lit up: "I am very rich. I am rich because of the suffering I have endured. Every time something hurts me, a movement begins within me, and usually, after that, a new awareness is born, leading to growth. I have discovered treasures within my pain."

In her darkness, she had found treasure and reached a reconciliation with the totality of life. Both joys and successes, as well as pains and darkness, had taken on meaning for her.

Mahsa was a friend I had met only recently. She was a hardworking woman who, despite her maternal duties, was very active and successful in both her studies and career. However, she often blamed herself for not being able to follow her plans. She asked me to help her work through this issue, and the outcome she ultimately reached was both interesting and surprising. Mahsa realized that when she tries to execute her desired plans but encounters limitations or uncontrollable events, she should trust the flow of events, accept what happens, and go with the flow.

Months later, I met Mahsa at a conference. She had traveled a long way to attend. As I was about to say goodbye, I asked her, "By the way, where are you staying tonight?"

She said, "I tried several times to book a hotel room before the trip, but it didn't work out. I felt like existence was telling me to trust it and not book a place. Now, I'm just going to look for a hotel."

I happily invited her to stay at my place for the night, and she accepted. That evening, I realized that over the past few months, she had deeply cultivated surrender and acceptance within herself. We were both incredibly happy that she hadn't managed to book a room in advance and had trusted existence. This created a unique opportunity for a delightful conversation and allowed us to deepen our friendship.

I am immensely grateful to meet such wonderful people and to have the chance to be a mirror for them along their life journey, helping them see the greatness within themselves and find solutions to their problems through their inner wisdom.

What you seek is not outside you; Look within yourself, for what you want, you are.[1]

---

1. *Divan-e Shams-e Tabrizi* [The Collected Poems of Shams of Tabriz]. (Original Persian work).

In Search of the Meaning of Self

About the Author

Dr. Maryam (Elnaz) Rahimzadeh

is an inner transformation coach and self-actualization instructor certified by the International Coaching Federation (ICF). She is also a dentist and a graduate in business coaching.

Elnaz believes that human well-being and health depend on a harmonious connection between physical, mental, and spiritual health. This understanding led her, after years in the health industry focusing on the body, to embark on a new path to accompany people on their journey of inner flourishing.

Her mission is to support educated, diligent, and successful individuals who have spent years pursuing external achievements but are now seeking to return to their authentic selves amidst burnout, the pressures of social roles, and a sense of meaninglessness. She aims to help them recreate peace, satisfaction, and balance in their lives.

Elnaz's life story began with academic success, but after experiencing depression and the loss of her brother, she entered a deep phase of searching for self-knowledge, understanding the mechanisms of the human psyche, and finding meaning during times of internal and external crises. This search led her to discover how to create awakening and transformation from within suffering.

Elnaz deeply believes that humans experience the world within themselves and that creating a meaningful and fulfilling life requires an authentic connection with oneself, others, and existence.

Drawing on her clinical experience, psychological knowledge, and coaching skills, she guides individuals who seek not just success, but vibrant, connected, and meaningful lives.

If this chapter inspired you or sparked a question in your mind, feel free to connect with her through the following channels:

📷 elnazinbloom
✉ elnaazcoaching@gmail.com

Horizons Born of Dreams
Guiding Your Inner Journey

Dr. Farinaz Rashedmarandi

Horizons Born of Dreams
Guiding Your Inner Journey
Dr. Farinaz Rashedmarandi
Pathologist, Health Coach, and Business Consultant

I believe that our aspirations create the distant horizons of our lives—horizons that gradually unfold with time. When the results of the national residency entrance exam were announced, I was honored to be accepted into the pathology residency program at Tehran University of Medical Sciences. At that moment, a wish filled my heart: never to give a false report to a patient. This wish set me on a path that, not only advanced my medical expertise, but also empowered me to launch and lead new ventures.

How Did This Happen?

I found myself a seat in the conference hall at Sina Hospital,[1] where Ms. Zahra Khatami, a young biochemist, was speaking on quality control in the biochemistry laboratory. I was truly impressed by her deep knowledge and impressive expertise in the field.

At that time, comprehensive quality systems were not part of the curriculum for students or residents. During that short session, I realized there was an entire realm of knowledge

---
1. A general referral hospital affiliated with Tehran University of Medical Sciences.

beyond my reach. I wished I had the opportunity to speak with Ms. Khatami, whom was regarded as one of the leading experts at the Reference Laboratory.

I was amazed to learn that a diagnosis could be made while ensuring the process was controlled at every stage—before, during, and after it was performed. This realization gave me a newfound sense of the power to create change, which would later assist me immensely and fulfill part of my wish to provide excellent service to patients. The ability to complete a task while ensuring its quality was, at that time, a thrilling new perspective.

Around a year later, an extraordinary experience happened. I completed my residency and graduated, after which I was required to fulfill my mandatory government service. This obligation placed me as a pathologist at a location designated by the Ministry of Health for two years.

The Human Resources department at the Ministry of Health was bustling on distribution day. Young Pathologists filled the hallways, anxiously discussing the decisions that would determine their next two years. When my turn came, I entered a large hall where numerous tables were arranged, each staffed by representatives from different centers who were meeting with applicants. By chance, I approached one of the tables and introduced myself to the person in charge. He greeted me warmly: Dr. Mohammad Abbasi, head of the Reference Laboratory. The Reference Laboratory?! To me, it seemed less like a duty and more like the fulfillment of a dream.

The Reference Laboratory

The quality of today's medical diagnostic laboratories in Iran is vastly different from what existed in the early 2000s. The Reference Laboratory had long been recognized as a leading technical and scientific authority in quality control. Yet, at that time, many laboratories still relied on manual, often outdated methods, and standard procedures were seldom applied consistently.

Early in my tenure at the Reference Laboratory, I received a green book titled *Quality Assurance*. Its content captivated me so deeply that I could hardly put it down. I recall one day when a distracted driver hit my car on a street; while the police officer took care of the accident and insurance procedures, I remained entirely absorbed in the book.

The book offered a comprehensive explanation of what we now call process-oriented thinking: identifying the stages of a task, carefully mapping the workflow, defining team members' responsibilities, and planning how to trace and prevent errors from recurring. With great enthusiasm, I shared a summary of the book with a colleague at the Reference Laboratory. She listened quietly, then sighed and said, "I hope we can make it happen."

Eventually, a team of newly graduated specialists and I organized around the Comprehensive Quality Management approach and began to make steady progress. What developed at the Reference Laboratory during those years—gradually expanding and later adopted by medical universities across the country—was not an ordinary event; it represented a profound transformation in the structure and function of laboratories in Iran.

The Reference Laboratory, later merged with the Ministry of Health's Department of Laboratory Affairs and carried on its activities under the name Reference Health Laboratory, played a pivotal role in the advancement of the laboratory field by training and empowering specialists, and technical managers. For the first time, it also established centralized scientific oversight of laboratory performance.

A Training to Remember

I began my career as an assistant professor and researcher in the microbiology department of the Reference Laboratory, where I was also responsible for training both trainers and experts from medical universities across Iran. One memory that has remained especially vivid is of a young man from the National Oil Company who attended a two-week training workshop at the Reference Laboratory. I still recall his sunburned face and bright, grateful eyes as he approached me afterward. With sincerity, he said, "We work in the most remote border areas on the islands of the Persian Gulf. No one had ever thought of us before. we can now provide our patients with more accurate results."

When I Met the Master

I rushed up the stairs to the second floor of the main Ministry of Health building and entered the office of Dr. Kamel Shadpour,[1]. A man of modest stature with a warm, genuine smile, he welcomed me kindly and asked the purpose of my visit.

At the time, I was doing everything I could to turn the distance learning project for laboratory staff into a reality. Dr. Shadpour listened attentively. Thrilled by my enthusiasm for the project, he said, "My dear, you have a difficult task ahead. If you are determined, remember that this is a significant undertaking that requires patience and perseverance. You could have chosen a conventional career path, but instead you have chosen this one, and many learners will benefit from it. It is a seed you are planting, and one day you will look back and say, 'These are the saplings I have planted."

Despite a year of persistent follow-up efforts, distance learning could not be implemented in 2007 due to insufficient internet infrastructure. Nevertheless, my dedicated colleagues and I at the Reference Laboratory remained committed to advancing the quality of laboratory services nationwide through education, standardization, and benchmarking.'"

This new way of thinking fundamentally reshaped my

---

1. Dr. Kamel Shadpour, the father of Iran's primary healthcare network, was born in 1937 in Rasht. He was one of the pioneers and founders of the primary healthcare network structure from before the Revolution until the late 1990s. His remarkable contributions in the field of preventive medicine, the expansion of rural health services, and the design and development of healthcare networks remain enduring in the history of Iran's health system.

perspective on work, deepening my sense of responsibility, while also softening my, perhaps at times, overly strict approach toward colleagues. I have come to believe that when people clearly understand their responsibilities, they are naturally inclined to fulfill them. If that does not occur, it is often a sign either that the role does not suit them or that our expectations have not been communicated clearly.

When a Colleague Became a Challenge

There remained many things that I still needed to learn. Early in my career, I received a notice about a Neuro-Linguistic Programming (NLP) workshop led by Dr. Issa Jalali from the Medical Council. My husband and I both attended the ten-session workshop. At that time, I had a colleague at the Reference Laboratory whose behavior was very distressing and I had not yet found an effective way to resolve the issue.

I recall asking Dr. Jalali during one of the sessions, "How should we deal with a challenging colleague in the workplace?" He looked at me and replied, "Perhaps the presence of such people is meant to strengthen us." His words resonated with me deeply and prompted serious reflection. Even after 20 years, I have not forgotten that moment. It marked a turning point for me—from seeing myself as a victim to gradually embracing responsibility for my own actions.

Saving a Young Athlete

One of our important duties in the reference microbiology

department was the identification of microbial agents that could not be diagnosed in university centers. On my first day in the microbiology section of the Reference Laboratory, I noticed an anaerobic workstation that had been donated by the World Health Organization but had never been installed. At that time, anaerobic bacteria were cultured in only limited laboratories in Iran, usually using small containers known as anaerobic jars. These organisms were particularly difficult to identify, and no antibiotic susceptibility testing was performed. The methods were not standardized, and when an anaerobic infection was suspected, patients were treated empirically with antibiotics, without laboratory confirmation.

I set up the workstation and devoted considerable time to studying and developing diagnostic methods and antibiograms for anaerobic bacteria. One day, I received a call from Shahid Rajaei hospital requesting an examination of a sample taken from a young athlete's thigh abscess that had not responded to any treatment. As soon as I received the sample, I began my work. The bacteria causing the infection proved to be anaerobic, and I identified the appropriate antibiotics, reporting the results to the physician. Three days later, the doctor called to thank me warmly, explaining that the patient had fully recovered thanks to the accurate diagnosis and the treatment recommended by the Reference Laboratory.

The Magic of Books

Our house had large built-in closets serving as bookshelves, filled with my father's collection. There were novels, works of philosophy, physics, chemistry, and art—all side by side. To me, this space felt like a garden in full bloom, where I could spend hours immersed in reading. While I may not remember every detail of what I read, I know that something from those books has stayed with me, offering a quiet sense of familiarity whenever I face the unfamiliar in life.

Inner Peace

When I was 16 or 17, I stumbled upon a poem by the British poet William Blake in one of my father's magazines. At the time, I felt I was confronting a profound concept, but I couldn't quite grasp it. It wasn't until a cool, pleasant spring evening that I paused by a park and decided to step inside.[1] The wet, rain-soaked atmosphere drew me in and led me to the cypress trees. I stopped and gazed at the trembling raindrops hanging from the branches, their reflections capturing the beauty of the trees. It was an unusual feeling. For a moment, I felt disconnected from time and place. I told myself, "If I were to leave this world at this moment, I would surely enter heaven." But another voice whispered, "You are already in heaven!"

In that moment, the veil was lifted, and the meaning of Blake's magnificent poem[2] revealed itself to me:

---

1. Lavizan Park in Tehran
2. Blake, W. (ca. 1803). Auguries of Innocence. In *The Pickering Manuscript*.

"To see a world in a grain of sand
And a heaven in a wild flower,
Hold infinity in the palm of your hand
And eternity in an hour."

Hafez: The Solitary Sage

I sat in Rudaki Hall, waiting for Pari Saberi's play about Hafez to begin. My thoughts were tangled, weighed down by a hidden rage I could not contain—the sting of a friend's biting words and hurtful actions still echoing within me.

As the curtain rose, Hafez appeared in heaven beside his beloved, Shakh-e-Nabat.[1] From the very beginning, the Devil stood on stage, tempting the poet and seducing him into ruin. At a decisive moment, when it seemed Hafez might surrender, it was love that ultimately saved him.

This work stirred a storm within my heart and soul. In its wake, my distress dissolved, and I came to fully accept responsibility for myself. How do I conduct myself in the presence of others? Am I patient, centered, and benevolent enough?

The Astronaut Program

When I was in high school, I was fascinated by physics. I read the life stories of Russian astronauts—especially Yuri Gagarin and Valentina Tereshkova—and often dreamed of becoming

---

1. In Hafez's poetry, *Shakhe Nabat* (literally, "sugar cane" or "candy branch") refers to a beautiful young woman who became a symbol of divine and earthly love. In literary tradition, she embodies both the sweetness of human affection and the redemptive power of love itself.

an astronaut. One day, a family friend asked what I planned to study in university, and I confidently replied, "Mathematics." She gently responded that our country was at war and in need of doctors. I must admit, his words left a deep impression on me.

On the other hand, my father hoped I would study chemistry and eventually enter his field of work. From my teenage years, he would share complex work-related issues with me almost daily. Although I did not fully grasp the technical details of his profession, I listened with interest and even took notes at times. His conversations were so engaging that I often lost track of time. What captivated me most was his remarkable creativity in developing new products, his meticulous attention to detail, and his genuine concern not only for his employees but even for his competitors.

Eventually, I enrolled in the medical program at Tabriz University of Medical Sciences. During this time, my relationship with my father grew deeper as time went on. Yet alongside this closeness, an uneasy thought started to emerge: after my father, who would take on the responsibility of managing his business in the chemical industry?

A Message from My Father

The doorbell of our old house rang, and I hurried to open it. It was my father, standing tall. He embraced me and, in his calm yet authoritative voice, said, "Farinaz, you should take care of my business." I woke up, drenched in sweat. This was an important message from my father, who had recently passed away.

Undoubtedly, stepping into this field as a young, inexperienced manager while also pursuing a career in medicine posed many challenges. In the early days, I often felt exhausted, discouraged, and at times even unmotivated. Eventually, I made the decision to enroll in several management and coaching programs despite my demanding medical schedule—an experience that proved immensely rewarding.

Today, I can confidently say that our business, once a respected brand in Iran but in need of modernization, has been transformed into a modern organization. Alongside a comprehensive rebranding, we have guided product development in a more environmentally sustainable direction.

Artunity

My husband and I were waiting for the results of the cardiology board exams when it was announced that Mohammad had ranked first in Iran. At that time, neither of us had any intention of immigrating. I still remember something he once told me that I will never forget: "I know that with my talent, if I leave Iran and invest in myself, I can become a prominent researcher or professor in my field. But my true passion is to uplift the people around me here in Iran and move forward together—even if it means not becoming the most outstanding version of myself." Before long, he was invited to join the Shahid Rajaei Heart Center at Iran University of Medical Sciences, where he began his career as a professor.

In my opinion, the path to becoming the best version of

ourselves is not always predictable.

Why is it that, at a time when creative and talented young artists are eagerly crafting their own inner worlds, so many others remain preoccupied with their daily routines and pay them no attention?" Mohammad asked me this question on a cold autumn night, and I embraced it wholeheartedly. From the seed of an idea, Artunity began to grow in the winter of 2018—an art startup dedicated to identifying and supporting young and emerging artists in our country, while also making authentic, high-quality art accessible to our fellow citizens at reasonable prices.

Sustainable Peace: Cultivating Within, Radiating Outward

Today, together with my dear colleague, Dr. Mahnaz Aghaeipour, I am responsible for leading the pathology laboratory at Laleh Hospital. The knowledge and experience I have gathered over the years have finally borne fruit, bringing me closer to the dream I envisioned long ago. I am sincerely grateful to our professors and colleagues, whose dedication and expertise enable us to provide services in line with international standards.

As a pathologist and an entrepreneur, I have navigated a challenging journey. Along the way, my most profound realization has been that coaching, when guided by purpose and responsibility, can serve as a powerful means of fostering lasting change. I have come to believe that the most profound wisdom often comes from unexpected places—from the brief, yet powerful, guidance of a mentor who taught me to plant seeds for the future, and from a colleague whose difficult behavior served as a turning point toward personal responsibility.

These people, who helped me flourish and realize my dreams, all used coaching techniques, knowingly or unknowingly. It was within these very challenges that I discovered the possibility of creating deeper value—not only for ourselves but also for the community we serve. For me, it is essential that our actions follow a path that contributes to peace, grounded first and foremost in the recognition of our shared human values. When approached with humility and gratitude, I believe, the universe offers its support, and the pathways to growth and flourishing gradually open before us.

What has enabled me, as a leader and individual, to flourish amid volatile and often difficult conditions? Over the years, I have embraced full responsibility for my life, choosing not to blame others for failures or setbacks. I have also learned to make peace with what lies beyond my control. On the path to flourishing, the most critical factor is to listen to our authentic inner voice and to define our core human values—something I was fortunate to recognize early in my journey.

In my view, both the path by which we pursue wealth and the way we treat the people with whom we work and live are vital to attracting true blessings into our lives. I believe the world becomes a better place when individuals support the people and communities around them.

From my perspective, one of the surest ways to achieve inner peace is through an appreciation of beauty, art, and culture, while one of the most reliable paths to fostering peace in society is through coaching. To truly appreciate beauty, we must first be exposed to it. Consistent engagement with nature, the elegance of architecture, and the richness of great art and literature deepen our familiarity with beauty. And how can anyone who is deeply familiar with beauty fail to be at peace with themselves and with the world? My journey has taught me that the true technology for change is not just a set of tools, but a deep awareness of the wisdom and strength that already exist in the world around us. With this new awareness, we can move from unconscious guidance to a powerful, intentional practice, making sustainable change and achieving our full potential to create a life of purpose.

Horizons Born of Dreams
Guiding Your Inner Journey

About the Author

Dr. Farinaz Rashedmarandi, a board-certified pathologist in both Clinical and Anatomical Pathology, has served for fifteen years as an assistant professor and researcher at the Reference Laboratories Research Center. She is the co-founder of Farvardin Pathobiology Laboratory and Farvardin Novin Laboratory, and currently serves as technical director and head of the Pathology Laboratory at Lalch Hospital. In addition to her specialized work in pathology, Dr. Rashedmarandi has completed a professional coaching program and now also works as a health coach and business consultant in various fields.

Dr. Rashedmarandi is an energetic and creative leader with

a proven ability to unite teams around shared organizational goals. She believes that creating a safer world and reducing social inequality require both business owners and employees to focus more on the factors that lie within their control, and concentrate on improving the quality of their services in a supportive and responsible manner. Her approach emphasizes not only serving individuals who benefit from these services but also caring for the broader environment.

Beyond her medical career, Dr. Rashedmarandi carries forward her father's legacy by preserving and expanding his business in paint and protective building coatings industry. She has also played a pivotal role in supporting Dr. Mohammad Kazem Taraghi in the creation of the Artunity startup, and currently contributes as both a consultant and an investor in this artistic venture.

Her interests include sports, travel, calligraphy and singing.

Please get in touch with her by using her email or Instagram.

✉ fr_marandi@yahoo.com
⓪ Dr.farinaz_rashedmarand

Seek Within Yourself Whatever You Desire, for It Is You

Marjan Shams

Seek Within Yourself Whatever You Desire, for It Is You

Marjan Shams

Researcher, Professional Coach, and Instructor of Personal Development and Leadership

If You Are What Is Lost, Why Don't You Find It?

This profound and philosophical statement not only holds a special place in mystical traditions and classical Persian literature but also aligns with modern concepts of psychology, personal growth, and contemporary philosophies. It serves as the foundation of coaching as well. Coaching teaches that to achieve real and sustainable change, you do not need to search for solutions outside yourself. Your answers and inner resources are what lead you on the path of transformation and growth. A good coach does not provide ready-made answers but helps you discover the resources, strengths, and solutions that lie within.

In this journey, one can also draw inspiration from Socrates, the prominent Greek philosopher. Through his method of Socratic dialogue,[1] Socrates invited his students to seek self-awareness and truth within themselves. He understood that to achieve genuine change, one must know oneself and

---

1. Socratic Method, also known as dialectic or argument, is a method of discussion based on a series of targeted questions and answers; in such a way that initially there is agreement and cooperation with the opponent's position, then the contradictions of their arguments are revealed and using their own position, their claim is refuted.

find solutions from within. A similar approach is applied in coaching.

Coaching Starts from Within You!

Coaching is an interactive process in which a coach uses tools, techniques, and scientific models to help a client gain a deeper understanding of themselves, identify their goals, and formulate a structured plan to achieve those goals. Unlike counseling or therapy, which typically focus on resolving or analyzing past issues, coaching is oriented toward the future and personal growth. In this process, the coach helps the client tap into their inner resources and effectively overcome mental, emotional, or behavioral barriers to achieve positive changes in their life. Instead of providing ready-made solutions, the coach asks targeted and challenging questions that provoke deeper thinking and help the individual find their own answers and strategies. Thus, in coaching, the individual not only moves toward external goals but also takes steps on a journey of self-discovery and inner development.

Why Is Inner Search a Path to Sustainable Change?

In today's world, coaching has become one of the most powerful tools for creating sustainable change in life. One primary reason for its success is the emphasis on self-awareness and understanding inner competencies, which enables individuals to overcome mental obstacles and achieve deeper transformations.

Among the psychological models widely used in the coaching process is the growth mindset theory, developed by Carol Dweck. This theory emphasizes that individual abilities and intelligence are not fixed; people can grow and develop in any field through practice, effort, and the acceptance of challenges. In coaching, this perspective helps clients develop confidence and view every experience as an opportunity for growth and improvement, rather than dwelling on past limitations and failures.

The SWOT model[1] is another tool used in coaching to identify and leverage internal resources while recognizing external obstacles. This model helps individuals evaluate their current situations more accurately and realistically, leading to effective solutions for improvement and progress toward their goals.

Starting from Within: A New Path to Change and Flourishing

Some may believe that to create change in their lives, they need to change their external conditions, such as finding a new job, changing their surroundings, or building new social relationships. However, both ancient and modern philosophies emphasize that the first step toward any genuine change is transformation within the individual.

Coaching helps individuals identify and change thought and

---

1. In Coaching, SWOT analysis (an acronym for Strengths, Weaknesses, Opportunities, and Threats) is a powerful guide for deeper exploration in self-awareness and strategic planning.

behaviour patterns that have formed over time. Such internal changes enable individuals to view the outside world with a fresh perspective, allowing them to make decisions that lead to positive and sustainable changes in their lives.

Socrates and Coaching: A Philosophy for Awareness and Flourishing

In the history of philosophy, few figures have transformed the concept of "self-knowledge" from an abstract idea into a practical and interpersonal exercise as effectively as Socrates. Unlike many of his contemporaries, Socrates sought truth not through preaching or oratory, but through active questioning and challenging dialogues. The Socratic method, as it is known today, facilitates thought, doubt, contemplation, and inner discovery, rather than merely providing answers. By posing seemingly simple yet precise questions, Socrates challenged the foundations of an individual's beliefs, encouraging them to reconsider and build more informed and authentic bases of knowledge. This method established a type of philosophical dialogue in which the individual is not a passive listener but an active explorer of their inner truth.

This fundamental principle is also clearly evident in coaching: instead of providing clients with ready-made prescriptions, the coach relies on skillful questioning to invite the individual on an inner journey to discover answers, resources, meaning, and their personal path.

Intelligent Questions, Profound Awareness

In coaching, the question is not a therapeutic tool or solution; rather, it is a light to illuminate the dark corners of the mind and soul. Such questions, often open-ended, guiding, and thought-provoking, are designed to take the client beyond their current level of awareness and confront them with parts of themselves that have previously been overlooked or unrecognized. Cognitive psychology and behavioral sciences also confirm this role. Studies have shown that the right questions at the right time can divert an individual's cognitive circuits from habitual neural pathways and steer them toward creating sudden insights or "aha moments."[1] These moments of inner discovery occur when the mind is actively exploring, not passively receiving information.[2]

In other words, in coaching, the question is not only a tool for discovery but also a tool for transformation. Just as Socrates activated conscious unawareness in his students with his questions, the coach, with precise questions, guides the client from an automatic self to a conscious and selective self.

Socrates and the Secrets of Hidden Wisdom

Socrates said, "I only know that I know nothing." On the surface, this statement seems humble, but at its core, it carries a fundamental message about the nature of learning and

---

1. Aha moment is a moment when a complicated or ambiguous concept is suddenly simplified or clarified.
2. Kounios, J; Beeman, M. (2009). The Aha! Moment: The Cognitive Neuroscience of Insight. *Current Directions in Psychological Science.*

growth: every transformation begins with the acceptance of ignorance.

The same principle applies in coaching: the coach is neither a teacher, consultant, nor judge. They act as a clear mirror, using their questions to invite the individual to observe themselves directly. Socratic philosophy teaches us that the role of a coach is not to convey truth but to awaken the process of discovering truth within the individual. This approach aligns with modern concepts of transformational psychology and experiential learning.

Research in positive psychology has confirmed that individuals experience the most growth and resilience when afforded opportunities for "self-exploration" and "self-testing" in a supportive but non-directive atmosphere[1]—exactly what Socrates did in the streets of Athens and what coaches do in coaching sessions today.

Modern coaching, while benefiting from psychology, neuroscience, and behavioral models, is deeply rooted in philosophy. The Socratic method is not just a technique but an attitude toward humanity: every person possesses knowledge, power, and a path within themselves. All it takes is someone who, through presence, silence, and questions, invites them to explore this inner world.

Coaching is not a tool but a journey—from awareness to

---

1. Ryan, R. M; Deci, E. L. (2000). Self-Determination Theory and the Facilitation of Intrinsic Motivation, Social Development, and Well-Being. *American Psychologist*.

action. Its impact on an individual's life goes beyond solving problems or achieving specific goals; it fundamentally redefines the individual's relationship with themselves, others, and the world around them.

When Data Speaks of Transformation

Over the past two decades, numerous studies have demonstrated the effectiveness of coaching in enhancing performance, improving emotional intelligence, increasing self-confidence, and clarifying life goals. A survey conducted by the International Coaching Federation (ICF) found that 80% of participants reported increased self-confidence after coaching sessions, while 73% reported significant improvements in their personal and professional relationships.[1]

Additionally, an article published in 2016 in the Journal of Positive Psychology showed that coaching based on positive psychology approaches, conducted over 8 to 12 sessions, reduced anxiety, increased hope for the future, and enhanced individuals' sense of control over their lives.[2]

Another study revealed that individuals who participated in the coaching process achieved their personal and professional goals 40% faster than others, and their level of life satisfaction

---

1. https://researchportal.coachingfederation.org/Document/Pdf/190.pdf
2. Green, S; Grant, A. M; Rynsaardt, J. (2016). The impact of positive psychology coaching on psychological well-being, goal striving, and hope. *Journal of Positive Psychology.*

was also significantly higher.[1]

The Story of Awakening

Niloufar was a woman in her thirties, educated, a mother of two children, and the manager of a marketing team. Everything seemed well from the outside, but inside, a storm was brewing. Every morning, with the sound of the alarm clock, she would ask herself: "Is this really the life I wanted?"

She was caught between two roles: a mother who wanted to be with her children and a woman who did not want to lose her professional identity. She did not know if staying in her job was a sign of strength or a futile persistence.

In coaching sessions, she initially broke down and cried. But gradually, her tears and silence gave way to self-dialogue. Using tools like the Wheel of Life, Niloufar gained a clearer picture of her hidden dissatisfactions and prioritized values. She followed her decision-making path step by step with the GROW model.[2] Ultimately, through a cost-benefit analysis of each choice and listening to her inner voice, she made a decision that satisfied not others, but herself. Niloufar did not quit her job; instead, she redefined it. She reduced her working hours, started an independent project in her field of interest, and most importantly, rebuilt her relationship with herself.

---

1. Matthews, G. (2007). The impact of commitment, accountability, and written goals on goal achievement. Paper presented at the 5th Annual International Positive Psychology Summit, Washington, DC.
2. The GROW model is an acronym for four stages: Goal, Reality, Obstacles, and Way Forward. This coaching framework helps individuals to define their goals and set their practical plans.

Keyvan, a fifty-year-old manager with a brilliant background, had a heart burdened by doubt. He grew up believing that self-confidence is an inherent trait, not one that can be developed, and thought his share of this trait had always been small. However, his life required him to make important decisions, lead his team, and excel in senior management meetings.

Coaching became a mirror for Keyvan to see his mental patterns. He held limiting beliefs, such as "I'm not fit for leadership" and "I always make decisions late." When Keyvan wrote down these limiting beliefs, he realized how much they had guided his life.

Using cognitive-behavioral coaching techniques, Keyvan challenged his ineffective thoughts and gradually wrote a new story about himself. Today, Keyvan is not perfect, but he is more accepting, braver, and better prepared; someone who can stand calmly in an important meeting and say, "I'm still learning, but I am enough right now."

These stories are just examples of thousands of small changes that begin in coaching sessions—changes that emerge from within the individual, not through advice, but by raising awareness; not out of compulsion, but out of choice.

Coaching: The Key to Continuous Growth and Inner Transformation

Coaching provides individuals with the opportunity to see themselves more clearly. Through guided conversations, deep questions, and meaningful silences, individuals connect to internal resources that may have gone unnoticed before. This effect is not temporary. Unlike many counseling or motivational approaches that yield short-term results, coaching paves the way for continuous and sustainable growth by fostering change at the level of beliefs, attitudes, and decision-making skills.

One of my clients said, "Coaching was like finding a map in the fog. The paths were always there; I just couldn't see them."

The Role of Coaching Skills in the Transformation Process

Coaching is not merely the art of change; it is the science of facilitating transformation from within. At the heart of this process lie skills that, like precise tools, enable the coach to create a safe, informed, and dynamic space for change. These skills form the foundation of the coach-client relationship, each rooted in deep concepts of psychology, behavioral sciences, and humanistic philosophy.

Active Listening: Listening Beyond the Ears

Active listening is not just about hearing words; it involves receiving tone, silences, pauses, hidden emotions, and even what is left unsaid. This skill is grounded in theories of communicative psychology, such as Carl Rogers' theory, which believes that a person only changes when they are deeply heard.

In coaching, when clients feel truly heard and seen, their defensive walls crumble, allowing their inner voices to express themselves. The coach, by accurately reflecting what they have heard, helps the individual gain clarity through the dialogue.

Effective Questioning: Questions that Awaken the Mind

Unlike counseling, which sometimes provides answers, coaching thrives on questions—specifically, questions that open doors rather than lock them tighter.

Questions in coaching serve as tools for discovery:

- **Open-ended questions** encourage deeper thinking;
- **Exploratory questions** reveal hidden layers of beliefs; and
- **Guiding questions** maintain focus on action.

This skill draws inspiration from Socratic theory, solution-focused approaches, and models of analytical psychology. A well-crafted question, like a light in the fog, illuminates the path without defining it.

Creating a Trusting Environment: The Soil in Which the Seed of Change Grows

Change cannot occur without a sense of security. The human mind instinctively resists the unknown. Therefore, a coach must create an environment where clients feel accepted, seen, and valued, even in moments of vulnerability or mistake.

This space is grounded in non-judgmental presence and the principles of positive psychology, transforming the coach-client relationship into one based on trust, authenticity, and unconditional acceptance. Only in such fertile soil can the seeds of transformation dare to sprout.

Action Alongside Thinking: A Bridge Between Awareness and Action

Coaching, unlike purely analytical approaches, emphasizes the transition from understanding to action. While awareness is essential, it has less impact on change until it leads to action. In this process, the coach serves as a facilitator for "translating insight into steps." By using techniques such as SMART goal setting[1], designing actionable steps, providing feedback, following up, and offering support, the coach helps individuals move from knowing to doing.

The Coach as a Mirror, Compass, and Companion

Coaching skills are not just techniques, but a manifestation of a humanistic attitude that views the individual as capable, responsible, and on a path of growth. These skills help the coach to be not an answerer, but a questioner of transformation, and not a path leader, but a companion in its discovery.

---

1. The SMART model outlines that a goal should possess five characteristics: it must be Specific, Measurable, Achievable, Relevant to our values and priorities, and Time-bound.

Coaching: The Path of Individual Growth in Today's Complex and Changing World

The role of coaching skills in the transformation process in a world where the pace of change has outstripped human analytical capacity is more essential than ever. The future of coaching is a return to human authenticity, where education is no longer just the transfer of knowledge, but the acceleration of awareness growth; where management evolves into leadership of transformation; where success is defined not merely by external achievement, but through authentic and meaningful living.

Coaching can play a crucial role in redefining concepts such as success, leadership, satisfaction, and self-awareness, whether at the individual level, within teams and organizations, or on broader societal levels. The future of coaching is more humanistic, deeper, and more meaningful, as it is rooted in the rediscovery of oneself.

Final Words

Rumi, with a profound look at the human soul, says:

> Everything in the universe is within you,
> Seek within yourself whatever you desire, for it is you.[1]

This statement is not just a verse of poetry, but the essence of wisdom of existence and the quintessence of modern coaching.

---
1. Divan of Shams, Quatrain 1759

Coaching is an invitation to self-discovery; not to construct a better version of oneself based on others' standards, but to recognize the genuine self that has been forgotten, but has never been silenced.

Research in the field of positive psychology and neuroscience has indicated that humans experience the most motivation and resilience for change when the change comes from within, not imposed from the outside. In this sense, coaching is a path towards self-directed learning, the foundation of which are self-awareness, meaning-seeking, and connection with internal resources such as wisdom, intuition, and values.[1]

This journey is beyond previous maps and preset paths; it is a journey into the darkest and brightest aspects of existence, where fears, desires, shadows, and lights are intertwined. On this path, coaching is not like a lamp that shows the way, but rather like a mirror that reflects our true face in silence, non-judgment, and love.

---

1. Di Domenico, S. I; Ryan, R. M. (2017). The emerging neuroscience of intrinsic motivation: A new frontier in self-determination research. *Frontiers in Human Neuroscience.*

Seek Within Yourself Whatever You Desire, for It Is You

About the Author

Marjan Shams, holding an official certificate from the International Coaching Federation (ICF), a Master of Business Administration (MBA) degree, and expertise in interactive behavior analysis, personality identification, and behavioral etiquette, began her coaching journey with a profound and humane perspective. She has had the honor of attending the Flourishing Trainer Course, led by Dr. Shahab Anari, and continues to learn with passion and enthusiasm. However, beyond degrees and skills, it is the path that Marjan has taken: an internal and external journey to understand humans more deeply, the root of their behaviors, and the ability to transform them from within.

Marjan, the multi-dimensional author of this chapter, is both a mother and a wife. While living a family life, she is a teacher who, with passion and commitment, illuminates the light of learning in the darkest points of doubt.

Marjan's interest in philosophy, psychology, yoga, and mindfulness has turned her soul into a garden full of pure questions and awakening silences, and her love for playing the piano and horse riding has taught her that life is a combination of order, rhythm, and liberation.

She believes that a person is not a dim sun, but a light that sometimes hides in the onslaught of dust.

Coaching for Marjan is not just a skill; it is an invitation, a call to return to oneself, to listen to the inner voice, and to start a new movement from the heart of awareness.

Her mission is to create a space for informed transformation; a place where people can regain their authentic selves, organizations can revive with their human spirit, and development is no longer just a managerial term, but becomes part of our daily life.

Marjan connects self-knowledge and effectiveness, introspection and professional action, and the vision of growth and the tangible realities of life.

Ways to contact the author:

✉ marjanshams965@gmail.com
🌐 www.marjanshams.com
📷 Marjanshams

From Teaching to Coaching

Nasrin Teimoori

From Teaching to Coaching

Nasrin Teimoori

English Language Teacher, Professional Coach, and Flourishing Trainer

Life is truly beautiful; how wonderful it would be if people spoke and interacted with each other with contemplation, tranquility, and empathy.

Throughout my years as a teacher, I have consistently participated in various educational courses to gain new insights into education and training. These experiences have helped me teach more effectively, deepen my connection with students, and create a classroom environment filled with enthusiasm for learning. However, despite my efforts, I was never completely satisfied; something was always missing. It felt as though I was searching for a specific approach that could enhance the relationship between teachers and students and boost motivation and learning outcomes in the classroom.

Many students and teachers were dissatisfied with the existing conditions, often feeling as if they did not understand each other's language. By the end of the academic year, we observed a decline in the academic performance of some students, accompanied by a decrease in their motivation. Meanwhile, teachers faced job burnout and extreme fatigue. This cycle of dissatisfaction gradually caught up with me. Despite my deep passion for teaching and my commitment to my students, I no longer felt a sense of fulfillment or meaning. The feeling of inadequacy and the lack of desired results from my teaching left me weary and hopeless.

Until one day, I found myself out of school and decided not to return. Despite the insistence of those around me to go back to work, I had made my decision. I felt I had lost part of my identity and needed to search for it. Nothing could make me happy in school anymore. The books I had taught with love for years now seemed soulless and repetitive. The students whom I loved attended class with apathy and often came to school only out of obligation. There was not a day when one of my colleagues was not dealing with a disciplinary or academic challenge with a student. Complaints about disengaged and disruptive students frequently dominated teachers' conversations. Meanwhile, my chronic knee and back pain had intensified, adding to my struggles. Climbing the school stairs became a real challenge for me. I decided to seek treatment, and the only solution was knee surgery. I had to take medical leave to address my condition. This period of treatment and recovery created an opportunity for profound transformation in my life.

Getting to Know Coaching

After undergoing knee surgery and spending a few months at home recovering, I became acquainted with Dr. Anari's coaching and personal development courses. This experience opened a door to a new and unknown world for me—a world where I could explore my true self, my beliefs, and my fears more deeply. I realized that every person has their own abilities and inner power; we just need to be kind to ourselves and uncover our mission in this world by recognizing our competencies. Coaching introduced me to a realm of possibilities where I could rediscover the meaning of my existence, my mission, and my values. With the help of coaching, I was able to view my life values through a fresh lens, reevaluate my beliefs, and confidently declare with renewed enthusiasm: I proudly consider myself a teacher, and I believe that teaching is not only one of the most precious and genuine human professions, but also it is a fundamental mission on the path of constructing a dynamic and informed future that can help people create a meaningful life. When this mission is accompanied by a coaching approach, education does not remain limited to knowledge transfer; rather, it becomes an interactive, inspiring, and transformative process in which the learner turns into an active, responsible, and purposeful agent on the way to their growth.

The Role of Coaching in Personal Growth and Development

In recent years, the role of coaching in enhancing educational processes, particularly in English language teaching, has received unprecedented attention. John Whitmore, a pioneer in the field of coaching, emphasizes in his seminal book, *Coaching for Performance*, that coaching can be a transformative approach that guides language learners toward deep, self-initiated, and sustainable learning. Coaching serves as a crucial link between the current situation and the desired outcome. A professional coach, through active listening, effective communication, and insightful questioning, empowers individuals to harness their abilities to solve life's challenges, as no one is more aware of their problems than they are themselves. The essence of coaching is helping individuals flourish by cultivating their unique talents and capabilities to improve personal performance.

One aspect often overlooked in today's society is the necessity of being truly heard. People engage in lengthy discussions and arguments, yet many still feel that "I was not understood" or "it seemed like they were not paying attention to me." A key lesson I have learned from coaching is the importance of actively listening to the client. According to my professor, Dr. Anari, "A coach should hear what the client says and what they do not say." In practice, this means that when someone speaks to us, we should focus entirely on their feelings, body language, and integrity. We must allow them to express their thoughts fully, in a safe and judgment-free environment. It is crucial to make them feel seen and secure, rather than immediately offering advice or criticism.

If individuals consistently apply these principles in their daily interactions with family, spouses, children, friends, or colleagues, they will not only reduce daily stress and pressure but also create opportunities for personal growth and deeper connections with those around them.

"Wisdom is the reward you get for a lifetime of listening when you would rather have talked!"[1]

Coaching Skills in Education and Educational Communication

"A successful teacher is the one who plans not only for their speech but also for their silence."[2]

The mission of a teacher is to train individuals who believe in themselves and their abilities and strive to make the world a better place. Teaching is not just about transferring knowledge or skills; it is about instilling a lifestyle that encourages critical thinking and the courage to embrace change for a better life. From the moment a teacher enters the classroom until they leave, the teaching and learning process is in motion. A teacher's behavior, particularly in response to students' challenges and failures, can serve as a powerful model for them. How students navigate future life issues largely depends on their experiences and the lessons learned from their teachers' behaviors during their studies.

By learning coaching principles and applying these competencies in the teaching process, teachers can support both their personal growth and the development of their students' abilities. A teacher who utilizes coaching skills strives to create a safe and supportive classroom environment

---
1. Attributed to Mark Twain
2. Attributed to Carl Rogers

that fosters learning, self-awareness, and reflection on students' abilities, interests, desires, and concerns. This environment provides an effective platform for students' growth and performance improvement, directly impacting their focus, creativity, motivation, and academic success.

Non-Judgment: The First Step for a Teacher to Make a Profound Impact

The break ended, and I still had the cup of tea in my hand when the school vice principal announced it was time to start the next class. My classroom was on the second floor. On my way there, the stairs and corridors were bustling with students coming and going, laughing. Upon entering the classroom, everything appeared disorganized at first glance. However, with my arrival and the sound of the class representative inviting students to settle down, order was gradually restored. The kids took their seats and placed their notebooks and books on their desks, and of course, as always, some had forgotten their books or notebooks.

For a moment, I looked at the students to calm them. I was facing a class of forty teenage girls, each with their own culture and world. As I opened the class attendance list, my mind replayed conversations with colleagues and the school principal about student behavior, low grades, and the need to contact parents. This issue seemed to arise repeatedly. During the brief breaks between classes spent in the school office, I could hear teachers voicing their frustrations about students who often appeared unmotivated or undisciplined. In those moments, while I waited for my tea to cool enough to sip, I longed to escape that stressful environment.

Yet, as I checked attendance, I wondered if we could approach students with contemplation and without judgment. Perhaps this would improve education at schools and make it more effective. Instead of labeling and critiquing, what if we asked about the reasons behind their behaviors and offered them a space to be heard? What difference would it make to think with empathy? Each student possesses their own unique world, character, and dreams for the successful life they wish to build. It is therefore unfair to hastily judge or compare them based on declining grades or occasional misbehavior, or to force them into our own narrow framework of success.

This lesson, learned in the realm of learning coaching, profoundly shaped my perspective. If I entered the classroom with an open mind and without prejudice, I could foster better understanding and offer more constructive responses instead of quick reactions. Coaching taught me that refraining from judgment is not only a mark of respect for others, but also a reflection of our own intellectual and emotional maturity. A teacher who wishes to be influential must first learn to listen without judgment, observe closely, and then find effective ways to interact.

Active Listening: A Tool to Understanding and Trust

One day, one of my students arrived late to class. My initial reaction was to reprimand her as usual, but that day I decided to try a different approach. Instead of responding quickly, I smiled and calmly asked, "Would you like to tell me why you were late?" She hesitated at first, then quietly explained that her mother had not been feeling well that morning, and she needed to stay with her until she felt better. In that moment, I simply listened—not to respond or evaluate, but to understand. I realized that when students feel heard, a lot of pressure is lifted from their shoulders. My student not only developed more trust in me but was also able to calmly explain the reason for her delay and accept responsibility for her behavior.

From that day on, my belief in the power of active listening deepened. I realized that sometimes, in a safe space free from judgment, labels, or unsolicited advice, students simply need to be heard and seen. Creating such an environment can be a powerful foundation for effective learning. Active listening involves listening with attention and mental presence—a key skill that every teacher or educational coach must cultivate for professional success. This type of listening helps create an atmosphere full of trust, mutual security, understanding, and collaboration in the classroom, transforming it into an attractive and dynamic environment where genuine learning occurs. In such an atmosphere, neither the teacher nor the students feel tired or bored by the end of class; it's as if time passed unnoticed, because the classroom is filled with interaction, motivation, and the beautiful flow of learning. As coaches often say, we not only avoid losing energy in the process, but we actually gain it. The importance of active listening in school goes beyond mere words. This skill provides students with a sense of "being seen," a feeling that encourages them to try harder, boosts their self-confidence, and fosters a sense of belonging in the class. When students feel heard, they are more likely to engage in the learning process and take responsibility for their behavior and progress.

Some simple and effective ways to practice active listening include maintaining eye contact when speaking with a student, nodding to confirm understanding, avoiding interruptions during the conversation, and conveying a sense of trust to the individual. These behaviors send a clear message: "I am here to listen to you." Conversely, one of the most significant obstacles to active listening is when a teacher, while listening to a student's words, preconceives and prepares a response in their mind. This behavior can create a sense of "not being heard" and diminish the student's trust in the teacher. Ultimately, another key tool for active listening is the skill of questioning. Asking targeted and open-ended questions is part of the deep listening process. Such questions not only clarify the subject but also demonstrate the teacher's attentiveness to their students.

Teachers' use of coaching techniques, such as active listening and questioning skills, positively impacts student learning and performance. Active listening makes students feel valued and supported, which helps boost their self-confidence and motivation to learn.[1] Additionally, open and targeted questioning enhances students' critical thinking and deepens their understanding.[2] Research findings show that coaching, by fostering self-awareness, self-regulation skills, and internal motivation, can significantly improve academic performance.[3]

Effective Classroom Dialogue: From Questioning to Empathy

In coaching, questioning is a powerful tool for fostering awareness, responsibility, and growth. Open and non-judgmental questions encourage clients to explore their thoughts, feelings, and choices more deeply. But is there such a space in the classroom? The purpose of questioning is not to test or evaluate weaknesses but to collaboratively clarify, support, and discover. Instead of scolding, prejudging, and asking questions like "Why didn't you study?" or "Why didn't you do your homework?", you can create a constructive dialogue that leads to personal growth and a deeper understanding of the subject with questions like "What happened that prevented you from completing this exercise?" or "What do you think you can do to resolve this issue?"

---

1. Rogers, C. R; & Farson, R. E. (1957). *Active Listening.* University of Chicago Industrial Relations Center.
2. King, A. (1992). Facilitating elaborative learning through guided student-generated questioning. *Educational Psychologist,* 27(1), 111–126.
3. Kraft, M. A., Blazar, D., & Hogan, D. (2018). The effect of teacher coaching on instruction and achievement: A meta-analysis of the causal evidence. Review of Educational Research, 88(4), 547–588. https://doi.org/10.3102/0034654318759268

Questioning, when accompanied by active listening, conscious silence, and attention to students' emotional needs, can transform the classroom into a space that nurtures thought, self-confidence, and genuine learning. Providing constructive feedback instead of labeling strengthens learning opportunities and shows students that failures are also part of the growth process. In coaching, we believe that the right question can open the door to fresh insights. This principle applies equally in the classroom: a teacher who asks questions, remains silent at an appropriate time, listens, and provides empathetic feedback not only imparts knowledge but also fosters human growth.

The Power of Coaching in Education: An Inner Journey for Transformation and Growth

This chapter offers a brief overview of the profound and transformative impact of coaching in education. You might think that educational counseling could serve as a suitable alternative to coaching. However, coaching is more than just a teaching method; it is a path to discovering identity, personal mission, and achieving sustainable growth. Coaching invites you to delve into the deepest layers of your existence and confront beliefs, fears, and obstacles that you may have never addressed before. This process leads not only to self-awareness but also to a commitment to personal and professional development. Coaching is an opportunity to set aside mental limitations and realize your inner potential.

Throughout my teaching career, I wished for schools to be not just educational centers but also inspiring environments for learning and creating a better life. I now believe that if teachers familiarize themselves with the principles of coaching, they will create profound changes not only in the classroom but also in their personal and social lives. Skills such as active listening, refraining from judgment, intelligent questioning, and attentiveness to the feelings of others transform teachers from mere transmitters of knowledge into conscious and inspiring companions.

Coaching helps teachers grow and transform in three key dimensions:

- **Behaviors:** By improving classroom management, planning lessons with clear purpose, and using effective teaching methods.
- **Beliefs:** By identifying and revising beliefs that affect educational performance and interactions with students.
- **Way of Being:** By enhancing their professional attitude, deepening self-awareness, and strengthening their positive impact on the learning environment.

According to scientific evidence, coaching as a professional development strategy plays a key role in boosting teacher performance. This process enhances self-awareness, increases motivation, improves teaching skills, and supports continuous learning, ultimately improving the quality of education and strengthening student learning outcomes. By focusing on individual growth, coaching helps teachers identify their personal educational goals and plan for their realization. It also enables them to receive constructive feedback, continuously evaluate their performance, and develop problem-solving skills.[1]

Extensive research has shown that the use of coaching techniques by teachers significantly raises student performance and learning.[2] Coaching increases student motivation and active participation while strengthening essential skills such as self-regulation, critical thinking, and responsibility in learning. Other studies indicate that coaching enhances self-efficacy and realistic goal-setting in students, leading to deeper and more sustainable learning. Additionally, coaching fosters an interactive and supportive learning environment, allowing students to pursue their growth paths with greater confidence. These findings demonstrate that coaching not only improves student grades but also cultivates lifelong learning skills.

---

1. Knight, J. (2007). *Instructional Coaching: A Partnership Approach to Improving Instruction.* Corwin Press.
2. Kraft, M. A., & Blazar, D. (2018). The Effect of Teacher Coaching on Instruction and Achievement: A Meta Analysis of the Causal Evidence. *Review of Educational Research,* 88(4), 547–588.

From Teaching to Coaching

About the Author

Nasrin Teimoori is an English language teacher, a professional coach certified by the International Coaching Federation (ICF), and a specialist in individual and group coaching for English language teachers. With a transformative approach to teaching and coaching, she helps educators turn daily teaching activities into inspiring experiences. She believes that integrating coaching principles with teaching not only enhances the quality of learning but also empowers teachers to discover their true mission in education with a deeper understanding of themselves. In her view, teaching reaches the peak of its impact when educators, in addition to imparting knowledge, inspire the discovery and growth of hidden individual talents and abilities in their students.

With over two decades of experience in teaching and training teachers, Nasrin has pursued her professional path with an unwavering commitment to learning and personal development. A turning point in her career was her introduction to coaching and flourishing at Dr. Shahab Anari's Coaching and Training Academy, which transformed her perspective on teaching and empowering educators. She is currently collaborating with educational institutions and schools to hold individual and group coaching sessions for teachers, helping them enhance their self-awareness, reflect on their professional beliefs, and develop their communication and instructional skills so they can play a more inspiring role in the classroom.

Nasrin holds a master's degree in English Language Teaching from Ferdowsi University of Mashhad and two internationally recognized certificates[1] in English language teaching. She continually strives to integrate the latest teaching methods with coaching principles and provide practical solutions to enhance teaching effectiveness.

In addition to her educational activities, Nasrin enjoys reading, music, tennis, and walking in nature. Continuous learning and sharing knowledge with others are her missions, as she believes that every teacher can be more than just an

---

1. Certificates in Teaching English to Speakers of Other Languages (TESOL) and Certificate in English Language Teaching to Adults (CELTA)

instructor; they can serve as a source of inspiration and bring about enduring transformation in the lives of others.

Ways to Contact the Author:

- Nasrin-Teimoori
- Teimoorinasrin
- Nasrin_coaching
- +98 915 303 4617
- www.nasrinteimoori.com

Published by North Star Success Inc.

 www.northstarsuccess.com

 support@northstarsuccess.com

 +1 647 479 0790

Write, publish and market your book with us!

We are experts in publishing with over 20 years of experience in the industry. We will help you bring your book to life and get maximum visibility, credibility and profitability with your book.

www.ingramcontent.com/pod-product-compliance
Lightning Source LLC
Chambersburg PA
CBHW061216070526
44584CB00029B/3858